FUTURE HUMAN BEHAVIOR

THIMON DE JONG

FUTURE HUMAN BEHAVIOR

UNDERSTANDING
WHAT PEOPLE ARE GOING
TO DO NEXT

Routledge
Taylor & Francis Group

NEW YORK AND LONDON

First published 2023
by Routledge
605 Third Avenue, New York, NY 10158, USA

and by Routledge
4 Park Square, Milton Park, Abingdon, Oxon, OX14 4RN, UK

Routledge is an imprint of the Taylor & Francis Group, an informa business

© 2023 Thimon de Jong

Library of Congress Cataloging-in-Publication Data

Names: Jong, Thimon de, author.
Title: Future human behavior: understanding what people are going to do next / Thimon de Jong.
Description: New York, NY: Routledge, 2022. | Includes bibliographical references and index.
Identifiers: LCCN 2022020146 (print) | LCCN 2022020147 (ebook) | ISBN 9781032129907 (hardback) | ISBN 9781032129914 (paperback) | ISBN 9781003227144 (ebook)
Subjects: LCSH: Social change--Forecasting. | Human behavior--Forecasting. | Civilization, Modern--Forecasting. | Future, The.
Classification: LCC HM831 .J664 2022 (print) | LCC HM831 (ebook) | DDC 303.4--dc23/eng/20220509
LC record available at https://lccn.loc.gov/2022020146
LC ebook record available at https://lccn.loc.gov/2022020147

ISBN: 978-1-032-12990-7 (hbk)
ISBN: 978-1-032-12991-4 (pbk)
ISBN: 978-1-003-22714-4 (ebk)

DOI: 10.4324/9781003227144

Typeset in Europa & P22 Mackinac Pro
Design by David Pino @ danki.com
Photography by Thimon de Jong, back cover image by Bram Willems

Publisher's Note:
This book has been prepared from camera-ready copy provided by the author.

Introduction   9

1. Blurring Realities

1.1 From external to internal filters   16
1.2 From post-truth to post-lie   19
1.3 Post-photoshop era   22
1.4 Blurring self-identity   28
1.5 Conspiracy culture   34
1.6 Double proof for the fact checkers   37
1.7 Loving black & white in a gray world   40

2. Trust Pendulum

2.1 Implosion of trust   50
2.2 Personal & informal trust   53
2.3 Bridging trust gaps   58
2.4 The open-source attitude   64
2.5 Be a pico influencer   68
2.6 Culture of appreciation & empathy   72

3. The 'You know Me' Society

3.1 Nothing on me   82
3.2 Digital James knows you   86
3.3 I know how you feel   90
3.4 Use my data! Fast forward to the past   98
3.5 Privacy paradox   100
3.6 My data, my € $ ¥ £   103
3.7 *Black Mirror* vs. Singularity University   106

4. Digital Balance

4.1	*Hate:* from technophobia to algorithm aversion	114
4.2	*Love:* digital addiction	118
4.3	Phubbing – ignoring people	126
4.4	The Future: counter trend, digital butlers & apathy	129
4.5	Digital balance as a luxury	132
4.6	Practicing patience in a world that's speeding up	138
4.7	The future of human work	140

5. Future Ethics

5.1	Who's responsible for this?	152
5.2	Jumping into the ethics vacuum	155
5.3	Ethics in the workplace	158
5.4	Moral licensing, purpose washing, and cancel culture	166
5.5	Puritanism fallacy	172
5.6	Indirect activism & nudge the nudgers	174

6. Mental Surplus

6.1	The normalizing of mental health	186
6.2	Gen Z: anxious activists	188
6.3	Mental health & technology	192
6.4	Suffering from home	198
6.5	Creating a mental surplus	204

Acknowledgements	214
References	218

INTRODUCTION

Welcome to *Future Human Behavior*, great to have you here! This book provides an accessible – and, I hope, engaging – insight into my endless fascination with how people are going to behave in the near future and what this means for organizations.

There is obviously a degree of uncertainty about the future. Distant futures (2050 and beyond) are often associated with science-fiction and crystal balls, but this book is about the near future: the next five to ten years. It is the future that is literally unfolding as you are reading this, and already influencing your decisions. Understanding it is necessary for anyone – and any organization – that wants to be fully prepared in the years ahead.

Let's start with a practical example. Imagine you're reading this book at Honolulu airport and you're about to board an airplane home after spending some wonderful days on the island of Oahu. When it's time to board, you walk up to the gate, where you are informed by the ground staff that your plane home will fly solely on autopilot. The cockpit door has been welded shut and the human pilots have been removed from the plane. The staff explain this is for safety reasons. They show you statistics that this century, more than 88% of airplane crashes were caused by human error[1] and that their autopilot software has more than a hundred billion hours of flight experience, compared to the hundred thousand hours of the most experienced human pilots.

Question: would you get on the plane?

The vast majority of people, myself included, would not, preferring to wait for the next flight. The one with human pilots. Or take a boat. Or better still, stay in Hawaii. I have used the above question over the past few years as a thought exercise with many groups of professionals. Although it is only hypothetical, it never fails to fire up a lively debate about decision making, trust, future technology and ethics. Interestingly, different generations tend to have different answers and opinions.

The follow-up question moves the perspective from the personal to the practical: what could the airline and/or aviation industry do to get people aboard their self-flying airplane?

This is not science-fiction. The autopilot technology is advancing so rapidly, the aviation industry is already considering how it can be effectively implemented.[2]

But though we understand the autopilot concept, how can we be persuaded to trust an entirely self-flying plane? To begin with, one needs to explore the rich (socio-) psychological research on people's aversion to new technology. Secondly, does the challenge of self-flying aircraft compare to other previous situations? For example, the autopilot dilemma shares similarities with the development of the automatic elevator.

The automatic elevator was invented in 1900, fifty years after the invention of the non-automatic elevator (which required a professional lift operator to manually start and stop it). The automatic elevator was a radical innovation and… quite a radical failure. People refused to get on them without an operator. Building owners thus refused to buy automatic elevators and the innovation failed.

Then in 1945, there was a six-week elevator operator strike in New York. It led to chaos in the city and building owners demanded a change. The elevator industry responded with a relaunch of the automatic elevator. This time however, they added a few features that were based on psychological research into human emotions.

The new elevators were equipped with a big red stop button, an alarm button, a phone connected to a support line and a full-size mirror. And as people were still anxious, the now much maligned elevator music and a soothing voice were added. It might be annoying today, but back then it relaxed us. Last but not least, the marketeers got to work, creating adverts with toddlers and grandmas riding the automatic elevator. Message: if it's safe for children and grandmas, it's safe enough for anyone. It worked. These additions won the trust of the public, and for most of us today's elevators hold no fears at all.

In retrospect, everything that happened in this historic case makes sense. But who could have predicted this great innovation would fail initially? Who could have predicted that a strike would accelerate public acceptance? Who could have predicted elevator music?

Understanding human behavior is key here: the response to new technology, how trust is built, the need to be connected to fellow human beings, how a crisis shifts ethical perspectives etc. These elements are discussed throughout this book, with key analysis of such fundamental themes as technology, trust, the perception of reality, ethics and mental health.

It is not a comprehensive book on the full breadth and depth of future human behavior. The carefully selected topics, research, cases and stories are inspired by fifteen years of working on future challenges with a number of leading organizations throughout the US, Europe and the rest of the world. Collaborating closely with industry leaders provided invaluable hands-on experience of the key future challenges modern businesses face.

The selected topics are the most relevant ones, which resonate strongly with both individuals and organizations, and – I hope – are the most practical and inspiring. That is my key intention for the book. It is not for specialists looking to acquire more detailed knowledge of a niche subject. It is designed to bring the outside world in, to introduce external threads and perspectives to a broad and engaged audience. To connect a few dots that were not connected before. As I have learned over the years, everyone can be inspired and challenged by different insights – I encourage you to find your own within these pages. Of course you can read this book traditionally from beginning to end, but it is written and designed to encourage browsing, dipping and engagement in an unprescribed way.

Cognitive science shows that people only remember 3% of the content of a book or a keynote presentation.[3] In my experience it's often even less than that – more like two or three *things*. To me this is not a problem at all, as long as the two or three things (being an insight or an idea) inspire a person to see something from a completely different perspective, help them become a better leader, or improve their decision making processes.

When I founded my company, I chose the name Whetston, which is Old English for whetstone – a sharpening tool. It serves as a great metaphor. I invite you to read this book as a sharpening tool to help hone your knowledge and your skills. Hopefully you'll find useful inspiration in the words and illustrations. You and your behaviors were my inspiration for the work that I do and to write this book. My thanks to each and every one of you for that!

Thimon de Jong

Addendum - Spring 2022

As I write the final words for Future Human Behavior, Putin has invaded Ukraine, to the horror and anger of us all. Much as I want to address these vital issues, it was not possible to analyze the longer-term impact of this invasion on the world, society, organizations and human behavior in this book.

It is currently unclear how this conflict will develop and be resolved. I have created a special virtual keynote as a bonus chapter for readers, where I delve more deeply into the impact of Russia's invasion of Ukraine. You can access this free presentation using the following QR code:

1.
Blurring Realities

1.1   From external to internal filters
1.2   From post-truth to post-lie
1.3   Post-photoshop era
1.4   Blurring self-identity
1.5   Conspiracy culture
1.6   Double proof for the fact checkers
1.7   Loving black & white in a gray world

INTRODUCTION

Since the 18th century, every generation has felt it was more well informed than its predecessors. And every time this leads to feelings of information overload, that this is just too much information to cope with – not just for individuals, but also for society as a whole. Yet humans and society are very flexible and relatively quickly adapt to new amounts of information.

In the first two decades of this century, the amount of data and information to which the average human (with an internet connection) had access, grew exponentially. Going into the 2020s, there are two billion websites on the internet, containing forty zettabytes of data[1] (one zettabyte equals one billion terabytes). To some this is a not a sign of information overload, but a true infopocalypse.

In the 2010s people responded to this by seeking comfort in filter bubbles: pockets of selected information (and media) that could be consumed with ease. Preferably with like-minded people and with the help of algorithms that made a manageable selection. The Covid pandemic, with its prolonged lockdowns, drove people's screen time to unprecedented record highs, where the comfortable filter bubbles are omnipresent and available 24/7. Everybody in their own bubble with their own reality.

Even with all these information bubbles, quite paradoxically, the lines between fact and opinion, news and entertainment, as well as true and false, are becoming blurred. The 21st century has been labeled a post-truth era – or a VUCA world (Volatility, Uncertainty, Complexity and Ambiguity) – full of fake news, 'alternative facts' and conspiracy theories.

Is that really the case, or is this just an emotion, a feeling we have, comparable to what the generations before us felt? Time to deep dive into our blurring realities and see if we can disperse the fog.

1.1

FROM EXTERNAL TO INTERNAL FILTERS

The start of the 21st century can be characterized as an 'unfiltered age'. On the internet, and especially on social media, any information could be posted. Anyone could put up a website, start a movement, upload a video and express an opinion. The start of the 21st century was all about (radical) transparency and openness, and the free internet was a wonderful democratic grassroots place, without any governing body or policing.

The old filters could be bypassed: the broadcast network, the record company, the newspaper editors. Some experts claimed they'd soon be relics from the past – power to the people! The advantages were clear for creators and uploaders, but problems soon became apparent for viewers/readers. How do I know if what I read and see is real and true? What is fact and what is fiction?

This might seem like an age-old question. From Plato's cave to the concept of hyperreality, and from Descartes' famous 'I think, therefore I

am' to the Matrix, people have been fascinated by the question of whether what we see and hear is real. A difficult question to answer when we no longer have filters in place to help us make sense of the world.

Before the internet, most information we received had already gone through a filter and usually these were expert filters; the newspaper editor, the book publisher or the TV show production crew. In the past, society was used to absorbing filtered information and it also came in bite-size chunks (e.g. newspaper, TV news). The quantity of news and entertainment was limited by the number of pages, channels or the physical size of a bookstore or library.

There are many advantages to an unlimited and unfiltered information and entertainment offering, and I don't have an opinion on whether it's preferable to the limits of the pre-internet era. What is important is the change it has had on behavior, as slowly, but steadily, people start to realize two things:

1. I have to be my own filter now, my own fact-checker. In the 2010s, people began to realize that not all consumer reviews were real, not all news stories on Facebook were to be believed and these beautiful Instagram posts were not a true representation of someone's life, that there is no editorial filter on this explicit message board. That meant people had to do their own fact-checking.

I have to be my own filter now

2. Doing one's own fact-checking takes time, energy and creates lots of uncertainty. Do I really have to double check all information I encounter? Maybe some filters are a good idea, but which ones? In the late 2010s, serious newspapers saw the decline in subscribers come to an end. In fact, some even bounced back enjoying a sharp increase in popularity, like the New York Times.

In education, schools have picked up on this, increasingly encouraging children not to believe everything they see and read online. How to find factual information online has become a fundamental 21st century skill. In the Netherlands it's called 'media wisdom' and this is being taught already in primary schools, teaching children not only how to find information, but also how to interpret what they find online.

Should we leave it up to individuals to decide if information online is true or false? And who decides that and who is responsible for moderating false information? And how? Is there a one size fits all solution for misleading political ads, false medical information, fake reviews, bogus social media profiles etc.?

There is so much false and hurtful information online, that the 2010s saw a sharp increase in society supporting some form of internet policing.[2] The big platforms like Twitter and Facebook developed algorithms and hired thousands of people to moderate their content. Still, a lot of content that should be removed slips through their filters. In the coming decade we will probably see quite a few initiatives around content moderation, but it's doubtful if we can fully prevent all fake reviews or all political propaganda attempts. Until then, we have to be our own filter, with a bit of help from the old external filters, the traditional players; because although they might have decreased in size, they are still there.

STRATEGIC TAKEAWAY

Being your own fact-checker is hard work and stressful. Leaders can start by being empathetic to both themselves and their people when they're lost in our post-truth world. A practical step is to empower people, making fact-checking (or data journalism) skills part of a learning and development program, especially for the decision-makers in the organization.

Fact-checking is a fundamental 21st century skill

1.2
FROM POST-TRUTH TO POST-LIE

Many people assume that more information leads to better decision making. Managers want as much information as possible to make important business decisions, but psychological research has shown time and time again that more information leads to worse decision making.[3] And yes, people have more information available to them than ever, but they also have more *mis*information available to them than ever. And opinions. And emotions. And beliefs. And lies. And alternative facts. A huge, confusing mix that has led to the start of the 21st century being labeled as a post-truth era, where we don't know what is what anymore. The Oxford Dictionary defines post-truth as 'relating to or denoting circumstances in which objective facts are less influential in shaping public opinion than appeals to emotion and personal belief'.

In a world where people are overwhelmed by information, they are inclined to turn more to emotions when they must make decisions. Why are emotions so powerful? In a debate, it's easy to doubt all the facts, because who knows if these are true. But it's hard to doubt an emotion when someone is genuinely angry or passionate about something.[4] Maybe a better term to describe our times is the 'era of emotions'.

The 2020s mark the start of what I call the 'post-lie era'. For example, during his presidency, Donald Trump made more false and misleading claims a day than any of his predecessors. His opponents focussed on all these lies, the *New York Times* even counted his falsehoods, but his supporters didn't care, it was his emotion they were attracted to. Confident, brash and with a joke here or there; it was not about what he said, but how he said it. There is a lesson here for future business leaders. They will increasingly need to be able to express their emotions adjacent to sound facts. It has always been a key leadership skill[5], however the need for it becomes more urgent in a world where reality is blurred.

But what if the emotions expressed are lies? In the post-lie era, thanks to technology, we will be able to assess if an emotion is real or not. We discuss the technology of emotion AI and its lie detecting capabilities in chapter 3. For now, imagine the lie detector functionality of emotion AI being used on political candidates in a debate, so viewers can see on a dashboard the candidate's truthfulness. Do they really care about certain groups of voters? Are they really planning to act upon a promise when they win the election? How would an AI tool like that influence public opinion? Today, the most 'authentic' candidate might win, but what if it turns out we can prove a candidate's emotions are fake?

One challenge here is that certain categories of liars, like the pathological ones, believe most of their own lies.[6] And if you believe your own lies, you're not lying when measured by emotion AI technology. If we struggle to tell a fact from a falsehood and an authentic emotion from a

false one, where does that leave society? Will the facts still reach people who have withdrawn into their own filter bubbles where likeminded people reaffirm each other's opinions? Several social media platforms are trying to break down the most extremist filter bubbles on their platforms, but currently we see these bubbles pop up on a different page on a different platform. We have to accept that the genie of alternative facts is out of the bottle. In this post-lie society, we will go towards a world with multiple truths for different groups of people in society – what they perceive as real is entirely dependent on their own personal truth filter.

Beyond the truth and beyond the lie, these truths will be fluid, dynamic and ever evolving. Because people change, perceptions change and so their truth filters will change as well.

STRATEGIC TAKEAWAY

In the coming decades, we will be subject to even more information and more misinformation, and in the resulting confusion people will find themselves attracted to authentic emotions, as these are harder to debunk. So, as a leader, don't be afraid to express emotions, next to solid facts. Be aware that AI is being used on you, to check if your emotions are authentic.

1.3

POST-PHOTOSHOP ERA

I grew up watching TV shows like *Knight Rider*, and as a young boy I loved the car chases and especially the car flying through the air. I knew that the car couldn't really take off and fly just with the push of a button. I knew there was a stunt team involved and quite often in the background there was a ramp visible that was used to get the car airborne. But it was still a real car. Nowadays, when we see a flying car on television or in a movie, we assume it has been created using CGI (computer-generated imagery).

Our response is the same for photos that are too good to be true, too beautiful. We suspect these to be photoshopped, enhanced, altered or completely fabricated. My personal fascination with this goes so far that when I am traveling with my family and we get treated to something too pretty, like a beautiful sunset over a Norwegian glacier, where the sky is pinker than pink, the mountains dark green, and the snow crystal clear white, I find myself saying to my wife, "If I take a picture of this, people will think it's fake!"

The 1990s were the turning point. Photoshop became so common and CGI so sophisticated that everything visual, whether printed or on a screen, could be fabricated. We moved to what I call the post-photoshop era. I am old enough to remember the pre-photoshop days where

people in ads looked quite real and the 'space-ships' in sci-fi movies were made of real card-board. But the generation of youngsters born from the late 1980s onwards know that every-thing they see on a screen or on paper can be fabricated; it is their normal, it's just the way the world is.

Photorealism is the holy grail

We can take this same shift and paste it onto the future. It is expected that the technology of augmented reality (AR) – an extra layer of digital imagery 'over' the real world – will mature some-where in the next two decades.[7] That means people will start to wear glasses or contact lenses that project a CGI layer on top of reality. And having learned from the infamous Google Glass failure, it will probably not be a consumer product first, but worn by professionals to im-prove their work, like police officers, healthcare professionals or construction workers. When we slowly get used to this technology, we won't be offended by it anymore and it will be absorbed into our daily life.

A parallel development is that of holograms, where no glasses or lenses are needed, and an image is projected in 3D by a projector or laser. Currently, this is very expensive technology and used only in controlled environments such as a staged concert or conference, where the light, stage and angle of viewing are all aligned. Holograms are also successfully used to revive dead pop stars. The 2010s saw stars like Frank Zappa, Tupac, Michael Jackson, Roy Orbison and Billie Holiday perform again, often with real (live) musicians, and fans willing to pay regular ticket prices to see their dead idols '(a)live' on stage. We will soon be unable to tell the difference. So why would Beyonce go on a world tour, when she can perform 'live' via hologram? Abba have only recently launched their new album as holograms!

A downward spiral of reality blurring ever further

When these technologies mature, we will see AR everywhere and that means we will get used to the blending of real and virtual. Many people assume we will be able to distinguish the reality from the AR visuals. I am afraid we won't. And AR images don't have to become indistinguishable from the real world for us to confuse the fake with the real. These two will blend into one quite soon, because of a neural process called perceptual adaptation. This is the ability of the brain to adapt to something extraordinary, especially alterations in the visual field.

Perceptual adaptation was discovered in the 1890s by psychologist George M. Stratton. He did a famous experiment on himself, where he wore so-called 'upside down glasses' to see how his brain would respond. These glasses have mirrors which literally turn the perception of the viewer upside down. He wore the glasses consistently for eight days. The first three days he was struggling, bumping into things when moving about. But on day four his brain started to adapt, the world appeared normal again and he could move around, read, work like he would without the special glasses. Only when he really concentrated did the world appear upside down again.[8]

It is to be expected that our brains will make the AR layer part of reality and see it as normal life.[9] All we need to do is see AR mixed with reality for a prolonged period of time.

How real will AR get? Looking at CGI visuals of computer games at the start of the 2020s, it gives us a clear vision of the future. Graphics are becoming so sophisticated that the casual observer might confuse the game visuals with a Hollywood movie or a real sports match. Somewhere in the near future computer games will get photorealistic graphics, where everything looks as real as real life. Photorealism is the holy grail for computer game companies.[10] But it does mean we will no longer be able to see the difference between a real Barcelona football match and one played on a gaming console. You might say, so what? But what if a first-person shooter becomes so real, it appears exactly like shooting someone in real life?

With computer games the photorealism is still a few years away but the deepfake videos are not. Deepfakes are videos that mix artificial intelligence with existing video material of a person to have them say or do things that look completely genuine. These are a growing concern, some say a minefield, especially in politics. With a deepfake video, it is possible to have a political opponent say and do anything.[11] The 2020s will be the decade where deepfakes become as normal as a photoshopped image is today.

The adoption of deepfakes in society will go in two phases. In the first phase we will see deepfakes of politicians and celebrities saying and doing crazy things. This can vary from a political smear campaign where politicians say the most outrageous things, to celebrity sex videos. You can find ample examples of both of these categories online already. The response of people to the first wave of these videos is that they will perceive the deepfakes as real – with all the scary consequences that entails. Society should expect an Orson Welles *War of the Worlds* scenario, where a radio play of a Martian invasion led to a nationwide panic in the USA in 1938. It is very likely deepfakes will potentially influence a few careers and elections in the near future.

The default will be viewers and listeners not believing what they see and hear

This software is already becoming available to the general public. We are about to be flooded by deepfakes and it will probably become its own category on platforms like Snapchat, Instagram, and TikTok. For example, I use the Mug Life app in my keynotes to show how you can make a video of someone speaking, based on just one portrait. If you combine that with Lyrebird's voice-cloning software, you have your own deepfake.

The second wave will be the more interesting one. Society will have learned from wave one, that okay, these deepfakes exist. People will view video images with the same skepticism as a 'too good to be true' photo and will get used to filtering and fact-checking these videos.

Already, there is software on the market that analyses videos to see if 'they're deepfake, like Deepware or similar software from Microsoft. The latter software is part of its 'Defending Democracy Program' to combat misinformation.

The other side of the same coin is that politicians will be able to deny video or audio material with which they are not comfortable. No one questioned the authenticity of Donald Trump's infamous 'grab 'em by the p****' footage back in 2016. Should the same footage come out today, it would be easy to cast doubt by claiming it's a deepfake.

The implications of the second wave will be profound. It is a continual downward spiral of reality blurring. It will give a whole new dimension to the job of factchecker. Any organization, and especially news media, will have to adapt. The default will be viewers and listeners not believing what they see and hear.

STRATEGIC TAKEAWAY

Fake videos and augmented reality will have a profound impact on society and business, as they will blur the lines between real and fake even further. Organizations and leaders will have to be prepared for customers, talent and stakeholders not believing the messages they put out.

1.4
BLURRING SELF-IDENTITY

In my old school photos, I have many bad hair days; there is acne and there is one where I have a sweaty red face as it was taken right after PE class. In short, they are just wonderful because they are authentic. But in the post-photoshop era, school photographers around the world have started offering a 'retouch service'. For a small premium the photographer will remove acne, reduce a jawline, whiten teeth, erase spring-away hairs etc.[12] Many parents choose to pay for this option, because "they want their children not to be embarrassed" about how they look and, of course, to share a perfect picture on Instagram.[13]

Let's fast forward ten or twenty years and imagine these children are looking back at their youthful photos. They will see a cleaned-up version of how they looked then, a photoshopped self-image. I am very happy with my not so perfect school photos. In twenty years will our children be as happy with theirs? Imagine a child asking: "Dad, what did I really look like when I was eight years old?"

School photographers are not the only ones pushing this retouching of the self. Perfect pictures are also being created by a variety of apps that use AI to create a more beautiful selfie, including Snapchat and Instagram. The 2010s were all about beauty filters to create the perfect picture of yourself. Photoshop experts offer retouch services on the internet, to create the perfect vacation photos for Facebook. Several phones, like iPhone and Samsung, now automatically smooth faces and have beauty levels you can set for your selfie; yes, by default.[14] The photos we have of ourselves are starting to look better than we do in real life. Joking aside, I am waiting for the first mirror that automatically fixes my look, so I don't get depressed looking at my reflection in the morning.

The question is, are these photos real or fake? Some call them 'fauxtographs' and see these photos as a synthesis between the fake and the real, as it's impossible to determine exactly where the real ends and the fake begins.[15] Is this a bad thing? People are hard-wired to want to look good. A fresh haircut, nice clothes, a layer of make-up and designer sunglasses – or at a more extreme level, botox, plastic surgery, hair removal, implants… isn't the retouching of a photo just part of the same process? Yes, it is, but the effects are different. In a wonderful study people were shown different photos of themselves; half were photoshopped to look better, the others were the real ones. People

Fauxtographs

were asked which photos were the real ones and the majority picked the photoshopped photos, convinced they were the real versions.[16]

It is no surprise that studies find the majority of adults edit their selfies to look better,[17] especially the ones we share, and that the photos we see on social media are not a real portrayal of someone's life, vacation or career. Rather, it is a parallel world, an exterior shell where we are all deceiving each other a bit, and we know it. These people are our friends, family members and colleagues, we know these people are not as pretty as their social media photos portray them. Yet research shows we still get depressed by it.[18] Quite paradoxical. And then there is also 'Snapchat or Selfie dysmorphia', a term from the world of plastic surgery, where patients ask the surgeon to adjust their body to match the image they achieved on social media with the use of photo filters.[19]

There is a counter movement where people are sharing visuals with the popular hashtag #nofilter (or #nocgi) to emphasize the fact that no editing has taken place and to receive praise. Although editing does take time and skill, most people really do prefer the truly authentic representation of reality.[20] When a photo is unedited, we can appreciate it for what it is, without the mind having to take an extra step to determine to what extent the photo is real. But of course, the #nofilter hashtag is being misused to label edited photos as real and research shows that 1 in 9 #nofilter claims are fake.[21] There have been several initiatives to find and expose these so-called 'filter fakers', but there is no technical solution yet available to separate the fake from the real visuals with 100% certainty. Will we get some smart AI in the future to do that for us – a lie-detector for visuals? In the short-term, most unlikely, but the search for real, authentic visuals will continue.

Many young people are quite torn between showing perfect photos of themselves and also wanting to share their true self online. Instead of mixing both, some set up two accounts; an edited, curated account for the outside world, and a 'real' one for a small select group of friends. On Instagram the latter are called 'finstagram' accounts. Paradoxically it stands for 'fake Instagram' but it shows more reality than the real one, called 'rinstagram'. And of course, in practice the images on the second account also turn out to be carefully selected to portray a certain image. In fact, we are all lost in a big real-fake-true-false loop and it's demanding a lot of mental energy, both from a producer's and consumer's point of view.

Real-fake-true-false loop

Brands are struggling with this as well, especially in their marketing. How perfect a picture should they create? Interestingly, most brands pushed hard for the perfect picture, especially when it came to portraying people - and already perfect models were edited beyond perfection, to sell their products and services. More recently, brands woke up to the fact that many consumers wanted to see real people and a more realistic representation of themselves.

Unilever's Dove was one of the forerunners of this trend with their Campaign for Real Beauty, raising awareness of the fact that the perfect images of women we see in ad campaigns are edited. Dove has been using real models since 2004, when they launched a 'No Digital Distortion' label, to be used next to photos. Other major brands followed. CVS Pharmacy launched the 'Beauty Unaltered' campaign. Several magazines supported the Photoshop free movement in the 2010s, like Seventeen, Teen Vogue and Marie Claire; models joined in the conversation and complained about being overly photoshopped.[22] Israel and France passed 'Photoshop laws' making it mandatory to put a disclaimer next to photos of models which have been physically modified – disclosing that they are not real photos.

What will we see in the 2020s? As Gen Z is maturing, it is expected the non-Photoshop counter trend will get more mainstream as the youngest generation has seen the Millennials struggle mentally with the pressure to be seen as 'perfect' on social media. With the maturing of this movement, it is expected one missing category will join as well: men. The non-Photoshop movement has been almost exclusively about the 'look' of women's bodies and the self-image of young girls. Men seem to be only a part of the conversation as consumers of these images. Here's a strategic takeaway: include men in the body positivity movement. Yes, with their acne, beer guts, bald heads and hairy backs.

There is some good news though. People lie *less* online to people they actually know in real life. When we communicate with people online who we are unlikely to engage with again, we are more prone to lie.[27] Research suggests there is a fundamental difference between online lies and face-to-face lies. The latter are often spontaneous, in the moment, and it's possible to see the reaction of the receiver(s). Online lies tend to be more carefully thought through and planned. Next to that, we can't see the reaction the lies invoke, so we have to best guess the effect they will have.

We want others to be real, but we lie ourselves

Although we prefer other people to be authentic and real online, we lie ourselves. The online world has made it easier than ever. We lie about our perfect vacations, our professional success (one-third of LinkedIn users lie on their profile, recruiters estimate this to be 80%)[23] [24] – but we lie most of all when we look for a partner online. The vast majority of people, between 55%-90%, lie on online dating platforms.[25] Mostly we lie about our looks and our age, but the main reason for lying is that we assume others are lying as well.[26] We lie because we expect others to lie, so we hold each other in a gridlock of untruths.

STRATEGIC TAKEAWAY

Leaders have to carefully think about the identity they project to the world. With current and future technology, the perfect picture can be created more easily than ever. However, it is likely that people want their leaders to be more authentic and less filtered.

EXERCISE

FINDING FAKE

Brainstorm with a group of people and try to find examples of reality being blurred:

Where in society can you find examples of people struggling with the difference between true & false and fake & real?

Then go beyond the 'now': what further aspects of life can be blurred? Anything goes, so have some fun!

This is one to be done over lunch or dinner, as it's a bit more philosophical than standard strategy exercises and the answers can lead to quite a few sidetracks and stirring of emotions. Initially, it's best to give one or two examples to get people started. In my experience, fake news and Photoshop/CGI are enough to get people going. If you need a few more (or would like a few answers), here are some pointers:

The more followers you have, the more popular you are, right? No. Followers, likes, and comments can be bought easily online. Current Instagram prices at so-called 'clickfarms' are: 1000 followers for $1 and 50,000 likes for $25. In an interview an owner of a site that sells these likes and followers stated that the fastest growing category of buyers are parents who buy Instagram likes and followers for their teenage children. You can do the same for LinkedIn, Facebook and Twitter as well. As more and more people realize fake followers and likes exist, websites have sprung up that can analyze someone's social media accounts and report accurately on how many followers/likes are real and fake.

A wonderful example of the blurring of reality is Auto-Tune, an audio-processor that automatically adjusts the voice of a singer to perfect pitch, perfect time and perfect tune; it even works when singing live. Invented in the late 1990s, it quickly became so popular that experts say it's now being used on almost all albums. Music critics and music producers have started complaining that pop music has become 'too perfect'. Auto-Tune was even used in the popular TV-show *X-Factor* to improve the voices of the contestants – until the news leaked. And yes, there is a 'Live Means Live' campaign with an accompanying logo to certify no Auto-Tune has been used. This campaign is endorsed by artists like Ellie Goulding and Ed Sheeran.

The days of the photoshopped model are almost over as in the 2020s the digital model will mature. During the 2010s, the digital model was a fun mini-trend on Instagram, but the models became so perfect that at the turn of the decade, the world's first all-digital modelling agency was launched, The Diigitals. The site works like a proper modelling agency, in which models have their own portfolio, social media pages and premium brands with which they work – and they look absolutely stunning. When I shared the site with my colleagues here at Whetston, one of them said Koffi was the most handsome man ever.

According to Forbes, counterfeiting is currently the largest criminal enterprise in the world and the total sale of counterfeit and pirated goods amounts to $1.7 trillion per year; more than drugs and human trafficking combined. Experts say 'the trade' is expected to grow to $2.8 trillion around 2025. The drivers of this trend are the online shopping platforms which are full of counterfeit goods. Many buyers are deceived, but many know very well that they're not getting a genuine new Louis Vuitton bag for $50 and are happy to order a counterfeit product from the comfort of their couch. And it's not just cloth-ing or iPhones; counterfeiters are selling fake new cars, as well as vintage classics, and more worryingly, fake medicines. To confuse the situation even further, some fake products sold on the black market are actually real, as the official supplier has secretly produced an extra batch. This becomes a USP for black market sellers with their buyers.

1000 followers for $1 and 50,000 likes for $25

The vast majority of people trust fake reviews (more on that in Chapter 2), so these get faked a lot. Several studies have shown that up to 70% of reviews are fake. Sellers go a long way to get positive reviews, actually giving away free products to real people who will write a favorable review. There are commercial organizations offering these services and Facebook groups who organize these deals. So these reviews are paid for, but are they fake? It might just be a great product. To help consumers who are looking for information, there are several portals where algorithms are being used to analyze reviews, like ReviewMeta or Fakespot. I used the latter on a hotel in London where I was planning to stay. Out of the 3000+ reviews it discovered, only 48% were reliable. I did pick a different hotel because of it. Of course, all the excellent reviews of this book are real!

Good luck finding more of your own!

1.5
CONSPIRACY CULTURE

Before the internet, if you had a crazy opinion like 'the earth is flat', you would share it with a group of friends or family members, maybe in your local bar after a few drinks. The response would most likely be a laugh, a friendly pat on the back, maybe a few counter arguments and then onto the next topic. Thanks to the internet, the whole world has become a bar. And no matter how crazy the opinion, people will be able to find like-minded people who support their beliefs, reinforce them and start a digital movement.

To complicate matters, much of the information put out by public or private organizations today has been carefully crafted by public relations professionals, content marketeers, lobbyists, press officers and external communication specialists. This group of professionals, whose job it is to influence the public/customers, opinion in favour of their employer, has been growing steadily this century and is expected to grow further into the 2020s.[38][39] Globally, the number of external communication professionals outnumbers journalists spectacularly. For example, in the Netherlands, these external communication/PR professionals outnumber journalists by a factor of nine![40] Yes, that is nine communication professionals for every single journalist.

Often these communication professionals act as a layer of defence against journalists. When Covid hit, photo journalists in the Netherlands were not allowed access to hospitals or morgues, so the visuals in the news media that represented Covid were those of people hoarding toilet paper and wearing (self-made) face masks. Several commentators have blamed the lack of realistic images as fuel for the rise of Covid conspiracies. If the same kind of realistic photos that appeared during the Ebola outbreaks had been available, they could have shifted more of the public opinion towards following the strict lockdown rules.[41]

Even before Covid, several academics labeled the 21st Century an age of conspiracy.[42] There have always been conspiracy theories, but it is hard to quantify exactly how popular these used to be throughout history, as up until a few decades ago, researchers did not regularly track them.[43] What we do know is that historically conspiracy theories have tried to explain strange or dramatic occurrences, for example the JFK assassination, the moon landing or the 9/11 attacks. These historical events were so emotionally shocking to some, that the 'simple' explanation of what happened was not enough; 'There must be more than meets the eye!'

This century, a new category of conspiracy is on the rise: conspiracy theory based on bare assertion. This is conspiracy without an occurrence or incident. It's about creating a narrative out of thin air — like for example Pizzagate, where Hillary Clinton allegedly ran a sex trafficking operation from the basement of a pizza parlor in Washington DC. Another new category is the meta-conspiracy theory; that is, the belief that the label 'conspiracy theory' was purposely created by the elites in order to discredit 'the truth'.[44]

New: conspiracy theories on bare assertion

Conspiracy theories are also increasingly used as a line of defense, to immediately cast doubt on an opponent. In 2019, after the killing of 50 people in two New Zealand mosques by a racist madman (who justified his deed by referring to several conspiracy theories), the conservative American radio host Rush Limbaugh immediately speculated that the killer was a secret leftist who launched the attack to damage the political right.

It's not only political commentators or confused people on social media who do this. It's a tactic that has been used by multinationals as well. For example, several industries paid academic researchers to cast doubt on factual research on climate science, thus fueling the mad debate that global warming itself is a conspiracy. One of Donald Trump's more infamous tweets was: "The concept of global warming was created by and for the Chinese in order to make U.S. manufacturing non-competitive."

So why are all these conspiracy theories so popular? Psychologists have researched this extensively and the most common driver is the feeling of a lack of control over various aspects of one's life.[45] People who believe in conspiracy theories also feel dispossessed, alienated or unfairly treated by elites or experts. In addition, they struggle with accepting chance, coincidence and randomness: everything must have a reason. Conspiracy theorists see patterns everywhere.[46] When Covid hit the world there was an explosion of conspiracy thinking. This was an ultimate 'no control' occurrence, an invisible virus that seemed to infect people randomly, with no cure and only partly reliable test methods. It rapidly shut down society, almost completely putting people in social isolation with plenty of spare time and only their devices as a connection to the outside world. A very, very toxic mix, as the conspiracy theories gave people a narrative that helped to make sense of why this happened to them. Conspiracy theories allow those who perpetuate them to believe they have the one true picture of reality and that everyone else is mad.[47]

During Covid, online content recommendation algorithms increasingly suggested harmful conspiracy theories, even to viewers not intrinsically interested in them. Conspiracy theories have been shown to be wonderful clickbait, and more clicks equals more cash. Silicon Valley is slowly taking responsibility and several platforms have blocked the most extreme conspiracy disseminators. YouTube has stated it will gradually change its content recommendation AI to battle harmful conspiracy theory videos and that it will become more accurate over time.

Luckily with societies opening up after Covid and people becoming very busy and social again, many of those distracted by conspiracy thinking have turned their attention elsewhere. I'm sure in the coming months we'll see that the vaccines were just vaccines and not microchips implanted by Bill Gates to secretly control our actions.

We do know the future has more than enough unforeseen dramatic events in store for us and the conspiracy reflex is lurking just beneath the surface in a world full of blurred realities. Organizations should not be surprised by a conspiracy theory hitting them as well. The Chuck E. Cheese restaurant chain (600+ restaurants globally) had to defend itself publicly when a popular conspiracy theorist on YouTube launched a video with the claim that the restaurants sold leftover pizza slices as new. Yes, that is one person on YouTube, versus a global company.[48]

STRATEGIC TAKEAWAY

With the further blurring of reality, we will see more conspiracy theories in the coming years – even with tech companies taking action to prevent harmful theories from spreading. Organizations will have to brace themselves and be prepared for one of these to potentially target their business. It's hard to predict the exact narratives of future conspiracy theories, but expect to have quite a few hitting companies, as our society digitalizes further. And if a lack of control is the main driver of conspiracy thinking, how can organizations give their people, their customers, their stakeholders or even society as a whole more of a feeling of control?

1.6

DOUBLE PROOF FOR THE FACT CHECKERS

Although the battle against fake news cannot be won indefinitely, the fight is ongoing and the profession of fact-checker – a job around since the 1920s – has become omnipresent. In the 20th century, these professionals worked quietly in the background, but the 21st century saw them step into the limelight, with dedicated articles, columns, and sections. Almost all quality news media around the world employ fact-checkers and sometimes even whole fact-checking departments. The magazine *Der Spiegel* from Germany famously employs 70 fact-checkers. Storyful, a social media intelligence agency, carries out social media contextualization and verification to "deliver clarity in a world of confusion… and to help our partners make sense of the world."[49] Politicians these days are constantly being fact-checked, sometimes even live while they are speaking.[50] It is possible to do fact-checking courses and study it at university (often combined with data journalism). More and more non-media organizations employ fact-checkers, including universities, NGO's, governments and multinational corporations.

But how do we know when a fact-check has its facts correct? During Barack Obama's second presidential run, we saw fact-checks that cast doubt on the veracity of fellow fact-checkers. Was this driven by a political agenda? *Time* magazine ran a cover story called *The Fact Wars*. This war is also one that can't be won, because we'd require a fact-checker checking the fact-check of the fact-check. And a check of that one as well!

Fact-checking the fact-checkers might sound logical in a post-truth world where one media outlet checking another might be seen as thorough research, but it reinforces the notion of a blurring reality where people have to be their own filter. All the fact-checking seems wonderful, but in the end, it is about people being responsible for their own thinking. Many experts, including Harvard professor and conspiracy theory specialist Nancy Rosenblum,[51] believe that parents and schools need to place more emphasis on critical thinking skills. We need to become critical thinkers, to be our own fact-checkers, to develop our own filter.

This skill is not only needed watching the news or scrolling through a social media feed, but also when it comes to making business decisions. It's no wonder that one of the main attributes associated with the much hyped 'agile leadership', is ambiguity tolerance. Can leaders deal with doubtfulness, uncertainty, and a lack of clarity? And then, rather than trying to solve the ambiguity as if it was a difficult puzzle, can they accept that there is no indefinite universal solution? This is a leadership skill that can be measured in assessments, and it can be taught

and improved; it is more part of someone's EQ than IQ. No wonder many experts suggest teaching children this skill from a very young age, as ambiguity – the blurring of reality – will only increase in the coming decade.

The proof precedes the subject that it's proofing

Organizations also have to prepare for customers who will check the facts, and businesses should realize that increasingly, they are being fact-checked. Many of my clients want to embrace transparency – that wonderful early 21st century buzz word – and more than ever, they

have opened up and are willing to share information. But how do their consumers know this information is real? I challenge my clients to deep dive into the minds of their customers and think of the steps a fact-checker would take. What sources would they use to find out if what an organization claims is true? My advice then, is to facilitate that fact-checking route, something I call 'double proofing'; if people are double checking information, you have to double proof that information in the first place.

An example of the latter is Salty Girl Seafood, which sells fish products in supermarkets. Each package contains a unique code, which can be entered on their website. It will then show the location where the fish was caught, the vessel that caught it, the gear used, the name of the captain of the boat, and all kinds of information on the crew, like age, hobbies, and family life.

Now that's a private company's initiative, but expectations are that somewhere during the 2020s the so-called Internet of Food will be rolled out globally: a common international data language, that will use blockchain technology so all foods and ingredients of a product can be traced.[52]

Facilitate double proofing

Another example is the so-called 'making-of' culture, a look behind the scenes to show how something was made. Making-of videos are especially popular. As viewers don't automatically believe what they see – a photo or a video – many brands have discovered that if, for example, they launch a making-of next to a new commercial, it will boost its authenticity and therefore its impact.

This used to be a reactive strategy. Brands put out a new campaign that was not believed by the viewers/consumers. Fake! Brands reacted with a making-of, to show the real aspects of a commercial. It is now operating an offensive strategy where the original and the making-of are being launched simultaneously, so viewers can immediately do their fact-checking. Many brands have already launched making-ofs and behind the scenes videos, before the launch of the actual campaign. The proof precedes the subject that it's proofing.[53]

A making-of is essentially double-proofing in action and it works so well that there have already been examples of making-ofs being faked. For example Roger Federer doing an insane trick-shot on a Gillette ad shoot – filmed backstage with what seems like a mobile phone. Federer admitted years later that it was fake.[54] So in essence we need a making-of of a making-of. And then a further making-of of that one. You see where this is going.

In the media, this move from reactive to pre-active is also known as moving from debunking to pre-bunking. In a pre-bunk strategy, one doesn't wait for the lies, the fake news or conspiracy theories to appear, but fights these *before* they grow and spread. Media professor Cherian George from Hong Kong University states that debunking is not very effective as people find it hard to change what they think they know. So, journalists have to pre-bunk proactively; by giving more context, more facts and thorough reports.[55] In this way they bridge gaps to an audience that might be vulnerable to the fake news narrative.

STRATEGIC TAKEAWAY

As people have become fact-checkers themselves, organizations have to 'double proof' and 'pre-bunk' what they say and do. That means facilitating the information gathering journey customers, employees, talent and stakeholders make, to fact-check messages from organizations and leaders. And as a leader, develop ambiguity tolerance skills to manage one's own doubtfulness and uncertainty.

1.7
LOVING BLACK & WHITE IN A GRAY WORLD

A common defense mechanism, against the ever-increasing blurring of reality, is an escape into black and white thinking. It divides up all the confusing aspects of life into a simple yes or no, A or B, and pro or con.

In psychology this is called 'splitting', a mechanism to make sense of the world and to resolve inner conflicts. It is easy, takes less energy and people process so much information that they love chunks that can easily be stored in a closet. If information is ambivalent, vague, gray and fuzzy, it means extra thinking is required to determine what it means. We develop splitting at a very young age. Infants start to distinguish a notion of good and bad in their early childhood and whilst growing up they gradually depolarize these two opposites.

But that depolarization is under pressure from popular culture. Most children's books and films divide the world up into good and bad: e.g. the good mother versus the wicked stepmother and the Force versus the Dark Side (*Star Wars*).

Most blockbusters present this good vs. bad narrative: *Lord of The Ring*s, *X-Men* and *Harry Potter*. Most religions do too: good vs. bad behavior, God vs. Devil, heaven vs. hell. As do many politicians. Remember George W. Bush after 9/11: "You're either with us, or against us."

News media do the same thing. They know their viewers love splitting, preferably on the extremes. So, what do they do when a topic like global warming is being discussed? They invite two guests who represent the two sides of the discussion. One would be a member from the IPCC (Intergovernmental Panel on Climate Change), an expert who explains the climate crisis is real; and the other one would be a global warming denier 'expert', who says it's all b****** in media savvy sound bites. The first expert represents 99% of the whole scientific community and the other 'expert' represents a handful of conspiracists. The problem is that the casual viewer sees a one-on-one, an equal battle between the two sides and arguments from both have equal value.

Black & white,
good & bad, true & false,
real & fake, win & lose,
us & them

Often people ask if new technology like AI will destroy us or will solve our world problems. This is in fact a so-called false dilemma because there are many outcomes other than these two extremes. The answer lies in the middle, "probably a bit of both," which is not an answer most people like to hear in this day and age.

Many leaders I work with struggle with this same challenge. Their people would like an easy black and white narrative about the way forward, a clear strategy in an uncertain world. But has a leader ever dared to say, "I don't really know what the right strategy is going forward, so let's try this?" Leaders take the black / white approach, literally. I have been to quite a few internal conferences where the walk-on music for the CEO is the theme music from *Star Wars*: dum, dum, dum, dum da-dum, dum, da-dum. The setting has to make the CEO a Jedi (the hero in the movie), fighting the baddies who are – you guessed it – the competition. The subliminal message is, we are good, they are bad. Black and white.

Dum, dum, dum, dum da-dum, dum, da-dum

The 2010s have all been about vulnerable leadership, made popular by psychologist Brene Brown. This concept is mostly defined as leaders being open about their vulnerabilities, personal failures, uncertainties and shortcomings. Although many leaders rationally agree with the theory of vulnerable leadership, I have personally seen only a handful of examples, primarily among younger leaders – yes, millennials. This is hopeful for the next generation of leaders emerging in the 2020s. To use some modern management lingo: combine vulnerable lead-

ership with agile leadership with leading in a VUCA (Volatility, Uncertainty, Complexity and Ambiguity) world, and we have a great starting point for a new decade of leadership. It will be a gradual process though, as young leaders will not all take leadership positions overnight.

STRATEGIC TAKEAWAY

The black and white narrative is attractive from an emotional storytelling perspective. We are hard wired to love the world being divided into two clear categories. But as the world is gray and diffuse, it is a false narrative, and the long-term effect is a loss of authenticity and trust and hence reality being blurred further. 21st century leaders can embrace some black and white thinking for trivial sides of business but should learn to embrace some ambiguity when talking about the real challenges society and business are facing.

2.
TRUST
PENDULUM

2.1 Implosion of trust
2.2 Personal & informal trust
2.3 Bridging trust gaps
2.4 The open-source attitude
2.5 Be a pico influencer
2.6 Culture of appreciation & empathy

INTRODUCTION

The subject of Trust is one of the fundamental elements of any relationship and it is such a rich subject. What makes someone trust a person? How do people decide what information is to be trusted? In what way does trust develop over time, and how does it vary in different places, cultures, and generations? All people want to be trusted, all brands want to be trusted by customers. Every organization wants a culture of trust, and all leaders want to be high-trust leaders.

Trust is the foundation of almost all human relationships, whether it is on a personal or professional level. One could argue it is the essential element for any society.[1] To quote the Dalai Lama: "Trust cannot be bought in a supermarket."[2] It has to be built up, it has to be earned and that is often a slow process. It's hard to attain and easily lost. There is not a one-size-fits-all recipe, so this chapter will explore several contemporary strategies for building trust.

The previous chapter on Blurring Realities sets the tone for the state of trust in society in the 21st century. Just as it's becoming harder to determine what is real and true – with the digital

world diffusing our reality in a variety of ways
– so is it also becoming increasingly difficult to
determine who and what information to trust.

I'm sometimes asked if trust can disappear
completely. Yes on a micro level, but no when
it comes to trust in general. Many experts, like
the author Rachel Botsman, compare trust to
energy. It might change form, but it cannot
vanish.[3] Trust is a fundamental aspect of society
and human relationships and will always find a
place and a form.

2.1

IMPLOSION OF TRUST

Let's start off with some bad news. During the 2010s, trust levels in society were low, very low. The past decade has been described as: Death of Trust, Low-Trust Times,[4] Trust Crisis, The Decline of Trust,[5] Trust Deficit Disorder,[6] and my favorite, Implosion of Trust.[7] All these terms indicate that societal trust in institutions, media, business, and science is low, and that we come from a magical place where trust was higher: the good old late 20th century.

Thorough research on the relationship between trust and economy demonstrates that throughout history, these two have a positive correlation; in a recession, trust levels in society drop, in an economic boom trust levels go up.[8] [9] [10] So it is more than logical that trust levels dropped globally when the financial crisis of 2007–2008 occurred. The International Monetary Fund (IMF) has concluded it was the most severe economic and financial meltdown since the Great Depression,[11] so for trust to also go into a severe crisis was exactly what was to be expected.

However, as the economy recovered and picked up during the 2010s, trust levels in most countries showed no sign of recovery; they stayed low, and in many countries, even decreased further. It might be tempting to see this as a specific problem of our times, but if we zoom out and look at the long-term data, we can see a trend. On average, trust in media, trust in government, even trust in other people, has been decreasing over the past decades –

a trend that became obvious when researchers started measuring trust levels, in the 1960s and 1970s.[12] [13] [14] [15]

What might be causing this? There are two answers: One answer is that globalization and technology opened the world up on a scale people could not grasp. Pre-1960s, most people lived within a small circle that they knew personally and in a society that, for the most part, changed slowly. They did not travel far or often and what happened in the rest of the world only came through to them in manageable chunks of information. With globalization and technology, their world expanded, their networks grew bigger, and increasingly they lived in cities where they knew few of the people around them. They travelled further and more frequently, from a daily commute to vacations on the other side of the world. Technology opened the doors to more information, different cultures, opinions, experiences; more of everything 24/7.

People still had the same number of close friends, but they didn't necessarily live locally anymore.[16] And because of social media and free communication with the other side of the world, people have an extended network of people with whom they are only loosely connected. Institutions, organizations and brands have become larger and more international, creating a sense of detachment. Instead of having a trusted personal relationship with an organization, people increasingly feel they are being treated like a number.

Low-Trust Times

Death of Trust

Trust Crisis

Decline of Trust

Implosion of Trust

Trust Deficit

The second answer to the question 'why are societal trust levels so low?' has been described in the previous chapter: Blurring Realities. In short, people do not know what is real and true anymore, so they are generally skeptical in their dealings with the outside world, leading to a steady decrease in trust levels across the board.

In the coming years, the drivers of society's decreasing levels of trust are still there. Even if we wish to do so, we cannot go back to living in small communities, having little contact with the outside world. Globalization is here to stay. Yes, we do see a nationalist trend sweeping the globe, driven by an emotional countermovement, a desire to close borders and be with our 'own' people - whatever that might entail in practice. But even in countries with nationalist governments which implement policies that go against the tide of globalization, we do not suddenly see a sharp increase in trust. In some, it is actually the opposite, and there is a further decrease in trust. For example, at the start of the 2020s, Russians led the world in their lack of trust in institutions.[17]

The Covid pandemic had quite the rollercoaster effect on societal trust levels. The short-term effect, in most countries, was an increase in trust in government that reached the highest levels seen this century. Next to that there was a sharp increase in trust in local communities of friends, family members and neighbors. People started supporting small neighborhood stores and found themselves helping out neighbors that they didn't even know before Covid. The longer-term effect of Covid has seen a decrease in trust in general, caused by the epidemic of misinformation on the one hand and the negative effects the prolonged lockdowns have had on people's mental health on the other. All the working / studying from home has had an adverse effect on trust: it is harder to trust someone connecting virtually via a screen compared to meeting someone in person.

When societies came out of the lockdown and people started to compensate for everything they missed – travelling, going to festivals, hugging strangers etc. – there was a short spike in trust again. The future suddenly looked bright and meeting people face-to-face again increased trust in other people as well. But as the memories of the lockdowns fade, so will their effects on trust, and we'll be back to where we were: a blurred realities world where the long term trend is for low levels of trust.

STRATEGIC TAKEAWAY

Our low-trust times are the new normal and larger, older (legacy) organizations will have to get used to the idea of being less trusted than they were in the past. This is especially relevant for older leaders who might long for trust to move back to the 'normal' level they took for granted when they were young. However, organizations will have to brace themselves and prepare for the fact that, in the coming years, trust levels are expected to decrease even further.

2.2

PERSONAL & INFORMAL TRUST

So, we live in low-trust times. Most leaders feel this to a certain extent, or they use deductive logic to get there: "Well, I know for sure we don't live in high-trust times!" This usually leads to the practical question of how to increase trust, in their organization and as a leader. They need to stop looking at trust solely from the perspective of a vertical axis; low trust at the bottom vs. high trust at the top. There is also trust on a horizontal axis. On this axis of trust, we have trust in the 'formal & institutional', and trust in the 'informal & personal'.

The last two decades were all about trust levels moving towards the personal & informal side. What did this horizontal shift entail?

It was a shift from larger, familiar and traditional brands, organizations, labels, institutions, and parties, to people we know and with whom we have a relationship - or with whom we perceive ourselves as having a relationship. Large, formal, anonymous organizations were considered to be untrustworthy, detached entities where greed and spreadsheets rule. Whereas informal, smaller and 'people focused' affiliations became connected to trustworthiness, care, warmth and personal attention.[18] In qualitative research people said more and more often:

"I don't trust the political party anymore, but I do trust that politician I saw in an interview. She said what I was thinking."

"I don't trust brand X that much, but I do trust the lady working there. She is a great person!"

"That so-called expert is probably paid for his opinion. I'll go online and base my purchase decision on what other buyers are saying."

Don't Google it, check a reliable source

Rachel Botsman, trust expert, explained this shift as follows; "Trust and influence are directed towards other people – families, friends, schoolmates, colleagues and even strangers – instead of towards the hierarchical elites, the experts or the authorities."[19]

'A person like yourself' was deemed as trustworthy as a professor or an expert who devoted their life to a topic or field

This was the driver of the early success of the sharing economy. People perceive themselves as doing business with a person rather than a company when they connect to Airbnb or BlaBlaCar (a ride sharing service). These platforms connect a customer with a person, a fellow human being, just like them. BlablaCar is famous for matching riders up according to the amount of 'bla' they do – meaning, how much they like to talk during a ride. It doesn't get more personal than that.

Though sometimes trust may be perceived as hard to grasp, quite a few leaders from large firms have told me that they feel trust moving away from their organization.

The research is in line with the hunches of these leaders. One of the most easily accessible long-term studies into trust is the famous Edelman Trust Barometer, a global study measuring trust for more than 25 years. A standard question in the report is: who do you trust most? For years, all around the globe, two categories of people were in the #1 spot: technical experts and academic experts. And that makes sense, because these are the individuals who traditionally know most about specific topics. But in the mid 2010s they had to share the most trusted top spot with a new category of expert. For the first time ever, a person like yourself, was deemed as trustworthy as a professor or a specialist who devoted their life to a topic or field. This came as quite a shock to many, but it's not surprising as this reflects the long-term shift in society, where trust is moving towards the personal and informal.

A few years ago, the Belgian government was so worried about citizens googling for health-care information that they started an ad campaign advising the general public not to Google health related issues. They bought Google AdWords for the top 100 symptoms and when people searched Google about their ailments, the top ad result read, "Don't Google it, check a reliable source." They also released a hilarious video campaign where a couple gets sicker with every dubious web page they visit at home. The goal of the campaign was to direct Belgian citizens to a government website with reliable health information.

Of course, a government website is a formal and institutional source, and the Facebook groups people use in their searches are not. The best solution would be a combination of both. An example of this is SoMeDocs (Social Media Doctors), a group of certified actual doctors (more than 3500 members) that fights fake health news on Facebook.[20]

Trump & Brexit were perfect examples of this shift towards the informal & personal. Trump beat Hillary Clinton by making every argument and every political battle personal; all his opponents received a personal nickname. He refused to play the game traditionally. He swapped solid political arguments for a range of personal attacks and quite extreme emotional outbursts. The Brexit referendum is a similar story. It shocked the world and experts were baffled by the fact that people appeared to vote against their own economic interests. British historian Sir David Wootton analyzed it as follows: "The people certainly were very well informed about all the disadvantages of a Brexit. Every day they were reminded about them by the Remainers. But they voted for something other than financial security. They wanted a sense of belonging and identity."[21] With trust expected to stay low during the next decade, this need for belonging will remain and may even continue to grow.

When the Covid pandemic hit, it had an immediate effect on trust and swung the pendulum strongly back in the other direction towards the formal & institutional. Within months trust in traditional media peaked and trust in social media had decreased. This was also visible in the number of subscribers, clicks and views of traditional media. In most countries, trust in government went up. In the Netherlands, my home country, trust in our national government was up to 40%, a spectacular increase. Trust in traditional experts peaked with virologists, immunologists and health specialists frequenting government press conferences and late-night talk shows. On the other side, trust in online bloggers, vloggers and influencers plummeted, which led to hilarious headlines like 'Celebrity Culture is Burning' from the New York Times.[22] And last but not least, workers who were on the 'vital professions' or 'key workers' lists during the lockdowns became heroes as they were the ones keeping societies afloat. When analysing the professions on these lists one thing is undeniable: the vast majority of these jobs are from the formal and institutional side.

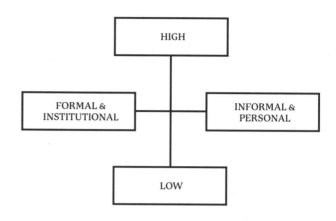

Celebrity Culture is Burning

This new found trust came as a surprise to many formal & institutional organizations and many did not act upon it as they were just too used to trust moving *away* from them. Some experts quickly drew the conclusion that this was an artificially inflated 'trust bubble' that had to burst once people became used to the crisis.[23] This was partly true – when the vaccine programs started and societies slowly opened up, trust started to decrease in governments and traditional media again; but a little extra remained. Especially for those governments, organizations and professions that helped and continued to help the world attempt to get out of the pandemic.[24] The expectations for the rest of the decade are that the pendulum will go back and forth. The shift might be towards informal & personal now the world is in a state of we-survived-the-pandemic-optimism; the next economic recession will most likely swing the pendulum the other way.

STRATEGIC TAKEAWAY

Next to moving from high to low, trust is also moving from the 'formal and institutional' to the 'personal and informal'. Trust here moves on a pendulum and leaders have to continuously analyze where this pendulum is and which way it's swinging. External events like a pandemic or economic recession can swing this trust pendulum (quite rapidly) in the other direction.

2.3

BRIDGING TRUST GAPS

Trust in society is not equally divided and comes in many flavours. This leads to multiple 'trust gaps' which organizations and leaders can fall into. But they can also use it to their advantage. An obvious and extreme example is trust that conspiracy thinkers have in business and government versus that of the general public. It is not that conspiracy thinkers have low trust here, they actively distrust the government and business: think of Pizzagate, blood-drinking elites and vaccines being a way to put microchips in our bodies. It is actually not a trust gap, but a trust Grand Canyon that is almost impossible to bridge. Only time seems to be able to bridge this gap: When the vaccine against smallpox was developed in the late 18th century, the antivax movement came up with the wildest theories against the vaccine: 'witnesses' reported that people who were vaccinated had their heads turned into that of a cow and others started mooing or grew cow horns.[25] This is now a laughing matter to all. And one day, we will look back and laugh about the mad Bill-Gates-microchip-Covid-vaccine theories that are making the rounds today. Other trust gaps are less extreme than the conspiracy one and sometimes bridgeable:

INFORMED PUBLIC VS. GENERAL PUBLIC GAP

In the late 2010s the gap between the informed public and the general public grew to a record high; when it came to trust levels, the latter had considerably less trust. The mass population is now more pessimistic about the future. They are more afraid of automation, job losses, and twice as many of the mass population respondents say the pace of innovation is too fast.[26] As most decision-makers belong to the informed public, and their peers do as well, they have to realize their own trust levels do not reflect those of the general public. Is this gap caused by the lack of knowledge & negativity of the general public or is it caused by the naivety & lack of empathy of the informed public? One for discussion over a glass of wine!

BUSINESS VS. GOVERNMENT GAP

In the 21st century, across the globe, businesses have become more trusted than governments.[27] [28] The paradox here is that one of the main reasons that governments have lost trust over the past 40 years is because they started acting as businesses, embracing economic liberalism with privatisation of the public sector, focussing on GDP and economic growth instead of well-being and allowing social inequality to increase with the dismantlement of the welfare state.[29] This has led to the general public shifting their trust to business and its leaders to speak out on societal challenges and be part of solving these as well. Peoples' primary concerns are simple – healthcare, education, housing, pensions etc. – and not something intangible such as Brexit. For businesses the trust put in them is also a challenge, as society

is increasingly looking to them to *lead* when it comes to world problems and not just make a great product or deliver a fair-priced service. We'll deep dive into that ethical challenge in chapter 5.

EXPERIENCE VS. EXPECTATION GAP

We put our trust in organizations on a daily basis and people have certain expectations when they do so. When these are not met by the actual experience, we get what's called an expectation gap and this gap can become quite large. In a global study, researchers asked respondents about their expectations and experiences with reference to 14 industries. There was an expectation gap everywhere. Media scored best with a small gap of 8%. Airlines scored worst with a 33% gap.[30] The latter has been the fuel for

several wonderful TV series that documented the micro cosmos that an airport can be; angry travelers, who were unpleasantly surprised by the expectation gap, were the main ingredient of these shows. The challenge here for organizations is that over-promising to gain trust can backfire when these promises are not met.

INDUSTRY GAP

There is quite a difference in the levels of trust the general public is willing to repose in various industries. At the bottom we find – surprise, surprise – financial services. Then we get all the other industries grouped quite close together, except for one. It is consistently the proud number one and trusted more than the others. Do you know which one it is? *Turn the page for the answer.*

IT IS TEC

INOLOGY

Globally, technology is the most trusted industry. Many executives I talk to are surprised by this, as *they* do not trust Facebook or Huawei. But the general public does, and with all the tech developments ahead of us in the coming decades, this is great news for the tech industry. They have to be careful though, as trust can be lost fast. Take for example Volkswagen's diesel-gate scandal, which caused trust in the whole automotive industry to plummet, and from which it is still recovering.[31]

Businesses are trusted more than governments

These trust gaps cannot easily be closed. However, it would be possible to build bridges across them, as organizations within one industry could work together to try and increase trust in the whole sector. Recently, two of Silicon Valley's biggest players, Tesla and Google, signed an AI pledge, akin to the Hippocratic oath in the medical world, promising not to develop AI for military use, i.e. it is not to be used for lethal autonomous weapons.[32] Time will tell if this was just window dressing or a really future proof, strategic business directive.

And wouldn't it be wonderful if the tobacco industries would sign a pledge to develop a non-lethal cigarette? Say, by 2040. Maybe that's wishful thinking by someone who has never smoked, but on the other hand – why not? This is an example of bridging the expectation gap that's easy in theory, but quite hard in practice. This is what marketeers do: reduce overpromising on the supplier's side and expectations on the customer's side. The good news for customers is that psychological research shows it will lead to a more enjoyable experience.[33]

STRATEGIC TAKEAWAY

Trust is not a one-dimensional topic which can be approached with a one-size-fits-all strategy. Depending on the industry and the target group, there can be more than one trust gap of which leaders and organizations need to be aware. These can complicate the building of trust. However, with time and effort, sometimes a bridge can be built.

Trust gaps cannot
easily be closed, but it is
possible to build bridges
across them

2.4
THE OPEN-SOURCE ATTITUDE

Now let's explore how to increase trust in practice. The first strategy is through new ways of collaboration. Over the years, 'collaboration' has become more than simply hype. It pops up everywhere; in conference themes, corporate values, mission/vision statements etc. What explains this focus on and love for collaboration? The answer is quite simple: our individualism has to be balanced out, it has to be compensated. In rich countries the prevalence of single-person households is at an unprecedented high.[34] We are job and relationship-hopping more than ever. We sit in our filter bubbles managing our own personal brand on social media. It's the me me me times where people expect instant gratification: IWWIWWIWI - I Want What I Want When I Want It.[35]

We are not hardwired to be so individualistic. It's our connection to our fellow human beings that makes us inherently human.

I have asked countless professionals to define their take on professional collaboration and the answers are always quite similar: "That's our X working together" where X can mean our teams, our people, our silos, our offices, our countries, our locations, or our business units. In my experience, collaboration is primarily defined as being collaboration inside the organization.

On rare occasions, customers and stakeholders are added as partners to collaborate with, but always defined as 'our customers and our stakeholders'.

There is another layer of collaboration that can be added, when looking beyond the classic Business 101 definition. I call it the Open-Source Attitude to collaboration, and it's best explained with a story:

A friend runs a small company in Amsterdam with 35 workers. Recently, he was looking for an intern. He or she would have to translate press releases from Dutch to Spanish, and a young grad student applied who ticked all the boxes, so they invited her to be interviewed. She had a great attitude and positive energy, so she got the internship. A few days after she started, she received her first press release to translate and she said to my friend, the boss, she'd start right away. An hour later my friend walks past her desk and sees she's not working on the press release but is doing something else. He asks her: 'Hey, I thought you'd be working on that press release. Is it all going well, can I help?' To which the intern replies: 'Well, I have a friend who is fluent in Spanish, and she is working on it right now. My friend does her internship somewhere else, and I am currently doing a little task for her.'

Pausing the story for a moment, let me ask you how you would have responded in that situation? I've asked many leaders this and the answers vary from outrage and fired on the spot, to excitement and promotion on the spot. So how did my friend respond?

First, my friend got mad. He accused her of lying to him in the internship interview, when she said that she could do the translating herself. The response from the intern to my angry friend was one of surprise: 'You will have the translated press release on your desk in an hour. What's the problem?'

There is a cultural element to this story. The Netherlands is known for its culture of flat hierarchy, where an intern can say, 'What's the problem?' to her boss after only a few days on the job. But putting that cultural nuance aside, the tale of this intern raises an interesting question for professionals: Is this behavior a problem? Is this a breach of trust between the leader and the intern? And practically, would your organization tolerate this attitude? Or would your organization encourage this kind of behavior?

I advise leaders to do the latter. I've discussed the story of the intern with several groups of students and most of them are agreed that they see the knowledge and skills within their network as available to them and part of their own: not their whole network, only the small group of best friends and family members. And my students agree that they would not 'lie' about it in a job/internship interview. Would they apply? Most of my students would!

It is in essence a corporate open-source attitude. If you'd like to use my knowledge and skills, here they are! Look at Tesla. The company decided in the mid-2010s to share all their patents, stating "Tesla will not initiate patent lawsuits against anyone who, in good faith, wants to use our technology."[36] The goal: to speed up the killing of gasoline fueled cars. A year later, Ford joined Tesla by open sourcing all its EV patents. And that move was followed by Toyota, who first shared more than 5,000 hydrogen patents, followed by 24,000 hybrid technology patents to be used until 2030 for free. Imagine wanting to start your own car company today and having all these EV and Hybrid patents free to use. It lowers the bar for any entrepreneurial start-up.

to renting someone else's place, they were reluctant to let out their own homes and apartments. The big problem being, what if my place gets trashed? Airbnb offered its own insurance back then, but who would trust the insurance promise of a foreign start-up? Airbnb realized they needed help and decided to collaborate with Lloyds of London, established in 1686, and one of the oldest and largest insurance firms in the world – the polar opposite of a small start-up. In this case, the heritage and size of Lloyds gave Airbnb the stamp of trust they needed. It was a wonderful trust marriage. Then they made a power move, upping the $30,000 host guarantee to a whopping $1,000,000 host guarantee – still backed by Lloyds of London. And this became one of the foundation stones of Airbnb's spectacular overseas success.[37]

Throwing in a few bean bags, table football and a casual Friday BBQ does not do the trick

Speaking of start-ups and collaboration, many of the legacy companies I work with ask me how they can create more of a start-up culture, as that is what talent seems to want. Their own large, old, dinosaur organizations need a culture which is more personal and informal; throwing in a few bean bags, table football and a casual Friday BBQ is not enough to do the trick. I encourage legacy companies to embrace the fact that they are old, large and institutional and see it as a strength. Don't try to be a start-up, just collaborate with them, because many start-ups could actually use a bit of formal institutionalism. For example, when Airbnb came to Europe in the early 2010s, it was still perceived very much as a small, untrustworthy Silicon Valley start-up. And although Europeans trusted Airbnb when it came

STRATEGIC TAKEAWAY

Having an open-source attitude means thinking about the knowledge & skills to which people have access, trusting and encouraging them to use this wisely and appropriately. As an organization, think of sharing information, even technology and patents, to move the entire industry forward and to gain trust. As for the larger legacy organizations, why not collaborate with a start-up instead of trying to become one?

EXERCISE

WHAT KNOWLEDGE AND SKILLS DO YOU HAVE ACCESS TO?

Sharing with a group of colleagues the knowledge and skill to which you have access, is a helpful exercise.

It will definitely lead to connecting to, and tapping into, each other's networks, and it might be useful for work challenges in future relationships. The better the connections we have with our colleagues, the more trust there will be in those relationships.

This exercise is best done in pairs. Each pair should be thinking as far as possible outside the box to create as many expert support links as they can. Give the group a few minutes to think or discuss with the person sitting next to them, and then share one example with the group. Many people struggle with this exercise as we are not used to thinking in this way. There are even people, always a bit older and always men, who struggle with saying their answer out loud - they feel ashamed, as if appropriating something that they feel is not theirs. And this is fine, demonstrating that generations do have different points of view when it comes to knowledge and skills.

The exercise often shows that while a group of colleagues, accountants for example, share roughly the same skills, the knowledge and experience to which they have access varies wildly. Some great answers have included:

– *Rocket fuel expert*
– *Leader in the field of transgender studies*
– *Private detective*

The key here is that the skills and knowledge we need might be closer to home than we think. Our first thought is often to type into Google, but perhaps our colleagues have access to the expert support or services we require.

This could have implications for the resume of the future. The typical resume consists of two pages listing our own knowledge and skills. Perhaps we should add a third page listing the additional knowledge and skills to which we have access.

2.5

BE A PICO INFLUENCER

Most consumer brands today have embraced the influencer as a marketing communication tool in a quest to appear more informal and personal. These influencers can take many forms: a Hollywood celebrity, a technical expert or an organization's own employees. The only prerequisite is the ability to influence the decision making of others.

As more and more brands and organizations started working with influencers, the return on influencer (yes, pun intended) has decreased. People realize that their heroes are being paid to promote brands on social media. The amount celebrities can get for promoting brands goes up to half a million dollars for a mention in one single Instagram post.[38] So, in the past few years, brands have slowly extended their influencer marketing strategies to so-called micro-influencers. These are people with 10,000 to 50,000 followers who are seen as experts or heroes to a smaller group of people. Because of the size of their following, their messages on social media are perceived to be authentic and therefore more trustworthy. As this strategy is also gaining (too much) popularity, several experts have predicted that the 2020s will be the era of the nano influencers. These are people with 1,000 – 10,000 followers and who are just like your own most popular friends and family members; their lack of any real fame will be a sign of their trustworthiness.[39]

The expectation is that this nano category will also eventually lose its authenticity and trust will move to the last category, the pico influencers. This is the category of people with less than 1,000 connections: the level of you, me and my neighbor with her dog. These are the people that we know in real life and with whom we have a relationship. The interesting thing is that we have then come full circle, back to where we were historically, when we trusted people who were actually very well known to us.

The principles behind a nano and pico influencer strategy are quite similar to the success of employee advocacy, which is the promotion of an organization by its staff members. In plain English, employees as influencers. Based on the research, it makes sense to use employees to build trust as the scope of influence of these employees is huge. As a thought experiment, let's take the average number of employees of a Fortune 500 company, which is approximately 52,000 people. These people all have diverse networks, so let's multiply the number of employees with a conservative network estimate of 150 people. This is the famous Dunbar's number, the amount of people with whom one can maintain stable social relationships.[40] Then we get a huge network of 7.8 million people. Even when we correct this for overlap of personal networks, it is still a huge sphere of influence.

Thanks to social media, the networks of employees can be reached easily and at little cost. There are several companies on the market that help organizations with this, like Hootsuite, Smarp and Everyone Social. How do they help? They offer dashboards that allow employees to post on social media platforms. These messages get tracked and pushed to colleagues who can then start to like, share and comment to give the original post a boost. All the activity of employees and the impact / influence a digital contribution has get logged. Most of the platforms work with gamification principles, like ratings and leaderboards and reward schemes, where the most influential employees get a bonus.

Influencer Tiers

Mega	1M+
Macro	500k – 1M
Mid-Tier	50k – 500k
Micro	10k – 50k
Nano	1k – 10k
Pico	up to 1k

The downside to this, is that there are cases where employers require staff to engage online and 'force' them to share things that the corporate communication team has cooked up to their personal networks. Some companies go as far as creating social media accounts for their employees – automated accounts that are in fact run by the marketing team. All these accounts then post the same content at the same time. From a cost perspective, this might be a smart strategy; from an ethical and trust perspective it's quite dumb, as these fake campaigns can backfire quite easily.

One of the pitfalls of many of these programs is that companies and the employee advocacy agencies they hire measure 'vanity metrics': the quantity of the posts, likes, shares, and followers instead of focusing on the quality of interactions.[41] But measuring this quality takes time and effort, while the quantity is easy to automate.[42] This is part of a bigger problem that we find ourselves dealing with today. The algorithms of social media just look at the quantity of likes, shares, and comments and these get pushed by the algorithm to the home pages and into people's feeds. The algorithms are programmed to perceive more clicks as 'better' content. But this results in so-called 'clickbait' being pushed forward by social media platforms and brands and influencers buying fake clicks, likes, hearts and shares from click-farms, where a piece of software or large groups of low-paid workers are hired to behave like actual people online. The goal of this is to influence the algorithms and convince consumers via the principle of social proof that[43] a product or service is great: look how popular we are!

The great thing about pico influencers is that the small size of their networks and realistic level of their activity is what makes them trustworthy. They are like you and me. And there is an important lesson here for large organizations as well: be human, be like you and me to build trust. The first is to communicate like a person. And secondly, adopt a 'flat-hierarchy approach' when interacting with customers.

Communicating like a person means an informal & personal tone of voice. Larger organizations often have this as a starting point, as 'authenticity' is one of the 'must-have' brand values of the 21st century. But what happens next is that the personal and authentic message go through one filter, then another filter and then some more, like the marketing communication department. What comes out the other end is a bland message that strikes the same chord as all the other filtered corporate messages.

Is it possible to strike an informal and personal tone as a large formal organization? JPMorgan Chase recently needed people for their blockchain team, but they failed to attract the right talent as they wanted hacker types – financial innovators from the fintech community. They decided to attract them by being very informal & personal in their job openings. Two lines from the job opening:[44]

"You have an opinion on Bitcoin and other cryptocurrencies, and you are probably ambivalent about the prospect of working for a large financial institution."

And:

"Sure, we are part of a large financial services firm operating in a highly-regulated environment, and that means we are not as flexible or agile as your average company – let alone a startup."

This is essentially a flat-out apology. I think the personal and informal tone is spot on and it worked. JPMorgan Chase got a team together, started collaborating with cryptocurrency hackers, and are currently future proofing and innovating for the 2020s.[45]

Many institutions have a culture of not saying anything negative or even reflective about their own organization

It's possible to even get more personal. A primary school in my hometown of Amsterdam was looking for a school director. Schools in the Netherlands struggle to find personnel because it is a high stress job that does not pay well compared to private sector jobs. This school decided to reach out to a group of candidates who would normally not move into the world of education: corporate leaders. They advertised in the FD, the Dutch equivalent of the Financial Times, and struck the perfect personal tone. This job opening got hundreds of corporate leaders to apply. How did they do it? I will quote the original copy – in full (translated from Dutch):[46]

Job opening: *School Director – we prefer candidates with no experience*

It's time for a long shot as it's hard to find a primary school director these days. So, we decided to look for one where no one else is looking. Right here in the FD between the power suits, brogues, and high heels. We're looking for mid-career fast-movers that can no longer ignore that inner voice saying, "What the hell am I doing with my life?!" If we can touch ten of you and then hire one, we've reached our 'target'. Yes, we speak the business lingo as well.

What do we need you for? To (finally) be the boss and lead one of the most fun primary schools in Amsterdam. We are looking for someone that has all the skills and capacities of a primary school director, but not the background. Simply because we believe in inclusivity, because we see that the world is changing, and the formal school headmaster of the past is not the school leader of tomorrow. We need to embed ourselves in society and in all honesty, we could get a bit more commercial, productive, and entrepreneurial.

This ad is a first step. And if you agree, we might be a match. So, grab your company iPhone and scan the below QR code to learn more and apply for a job with the most wonderful shareholders imaginable: 400 young children that you might advise to follow their hearts – sooner than you did.

That last line brought tears to my eyes, and I was so charmed I almost applied myself! Although quite different to the JP Morgan Chase advertisement, both are personal & informal and exemplify antidotes to our low-trust times. Unfortunately, many institutions have a culture of not saying anything negative or even reflective about their own organization, a culture that actually has the opposite effect: a decrease in trust.

clean. *So only three stars for Mr. de Jong."* Most companies can't and don't do this. But in the sharing / platform economy we do. Take Airbnb, where hosts and guests rate each other, or eBay where buyers and sellers give each other a rating. This has two positive effects: firstly, we behave better if we know we are rated and secondly, both parties give a higher rating, because the relationship is more equal. And we value an equal party higher than a subordinate or superior.[48]

"Mr. de Jong was a very friendly guest, but he left the bathroom in such a mess, it took us an hour to clean. So only three stars for Mr. de Jong"

A second strategy to being more human and more in tune with your costumers is the 'flat-hierarchy approach'. Put simply, the customer and the company are communicating as equals, as more equality leads to more trust.[47] Of course they are not literally equal, but the relationship is more equal than it was before.

A perfect example is that of rating systems. In the 21st century people got used to rating everything we do: the book we read, the movie we watched, the product we bought, and the vacation we took. We rate with likes, stars, hearts and comments. If I spend a night in a hotel, there are countless websites where I can leave a review about my stay. But there is an inequality in this review system because the hotel cannot review me. It cannot say, "*Mr. de Jong was a very friendly guest, but he left the bathroom in such a mess, it took us an hour to*

STRATEGIC TAKEAWAY

Trust is increasingly built via small personal networks (nano & pico influencers). Organizations can use their clients and employees as influencers, but they have to be careful not to formalize this and try to win the vanity metrics game. Leaders and corporations can increase trust by striking a very personal tone and not filter their messages.

2.6
CULTURE OF APPRECIATION & EMPATHY

When asked about how to become a high-trust leader in our low-trust times, I often reply, "What kind of leadership style do you have? Are you more of a formal, institutional leader or are you an informal, personal leader *as well*?" I consider formal and institutional leadership to be the foundation of leadership – I define it as the IQ side: the management side of leadership, quantifying performance, KPIs and managing everything that can be put into an Excel sheet. But how informal & personal are you as a leader? How is your EQ side developed?

Is this important? Yes. During the 2010s two large surveys (400,000 people in 190+ countries) showed that the global number one job preference of workers was "good relationships with my colleagues."[49] This should come as no surprise as, and I am repeating myself here, it's our relationships with others that make us human. So future proof leaders have to proactively think about how they can improve work relationships. They need their EQ skills – the personal informal side – for this and a focus on creating a high-trust culture where relationships can foster. But how to do that in practice? I'll give two examples of effective strategies.

The first is to create a culture of appreciation. People want their work to have value and preferably have value to someone. If leaders and colleagues express appreciation (or recognition) it means their work has value for the organization and they have value for the other person. Expressing appreciation improves a relationship and trust in the relationship will increase. Neuroscientists can even measure this process in the brain – appreciation has a positive effect on trust.[50]

I appreciate what you have to say

But how to get a culture of appreciation off the ground? Simple: just start. And please don't do this just once a year in the annual performance review. I often quote The Boston Consultancy Group, which advises daily appreciation. That's right: daily appreciation.[51] Most leaders I work with react quite strongly upon hearing this, saying things like:

- "Once a month would already be too much for me!"
- "My people know what they are good at, it's my role to tell them where they can improve."
- "If I appreciate them daily, they'll get lazy and less productive."

These responses are all fallacies. Yes, it is quite a step to suddenly start appreciating colleagues in an authentic way. Appreciation has to be sincere. But it is helpful to know that appreciation can take two forms. The first is a compliment. By giving a compliment, you not only make people happier, you increase your own happiness as well. It's a win-win.

The second is asking for someone's opinion. Because by doing so, you convey that you appreciate what they have to say. The great thing about asking for someone's opinion is that everyone can do this in almost any situation. The hard thing is, that just asking is not enough, it also means you have to listen to the answer. Practice active listening; you need to understand, respond, take the message seriously and then remember what is being said. [52][53][54]

That leads to the second way of increasing trust and that is by creating a culture of empathy. Like appreciation, empathy is key to strong relationships and helps to establish high-trust relationships and a high-trust culture. In my experience many people struggle with the exact definition of empathy, so here's a simple straightforward definition:

"Empathy is the process of demonstrating an accurate, non-judgmental understanding of the other side's needs, issues and perspective."

I've highlighted two words as empathy is about *demonstrating* that you *understand* the other person. It's not about sympathising or agreeing with someone else. Empathy is not a fixed personality trait, but it is a skill that can be learned. The FBI's critical response unit sees empathy as its most fundamental tool in hostage negotiations and they use it all the time to build trust in high pressure situations. They have even given it a cool name: 'tactical empathy'.[55]

The best way to do this is through active and reflective listening. There are shelves full of books on this, but there are a few basic dos and don'ts. The dos are simple: just listen to the other person. If there is a pause, don't answer; just be silent (count to ten in silence, that helps). Encourage the other person to continue to speak by saying "hmmmm", "tell me more" or repeating their last words. If they've finished, summarise what they have said to check if you understood them correctly.

When talent leaves, many leaders respond like a betrayed lover

The don'ts are much harder, especially for leaders. Don't interrupt the other person. There is a famous study where researchers looked at how long it takes before physicians interrupt patients when they first start to explain the reason for coming in. The average was a whopping 11 seconds and it sent a shockwave through the medical world, even leading to guidelines for doctors to listen to their patients longer.[56] Keep this in mind the next time you interrupt a team member. Another don't is to not judge unless you are asked to do so. The same goes for the hardest don't: do not problem solve. This does not improve trust, it leads to the other person feeling incapable. Often there is no need for problem solving at all. And last but not least, don't *say* 'I understand', *show* that you

The FBI's critical response
unit sees empathy as its most
fundamental tool in hostage
negotiations

understand by summarising their words. Then, and only then, can you ask: would you like my help/opinion/advice?

With this culture of appreciation and empathy, relationships in organizations will improve and people will be happier. There is a positive correlation between happiness at work and productivity, so by being appreciative and empathetic you will boost productivity – which looks great on that Excel sheet.

Take the opposite approach: embrace the job hopping of talent by facilitating it

A pro tip is to broaden the scope appreciation and empathy to ex-colleagues. Work relationships are getting shorter; in Europe, the average worker only spends a few years working at an employer. The life-long contract, working for one employer, has become an exception instead of the rule.

I am often asked, "How do we stop our talent leaving after only a few years? We invest so much time and energy in them and still they leave!" Many individual leaders respond like betrayed lovers, especially when young talent leaves – in their opinion, way too soon. A young leader in an ICT firm told me the story of one of his direct colleagues leaving the company to work for a competitor. The leader of that team then forced the team to remove that ex-colleague as a connection from LinkedIn as a 'punishment'.

My advice would be to take the opposite approach, not only to embrace the job hopping

of talent but express empathy and appreciation by facilitating it. Young people build their careers by working a few months here and a few years there.[57] [58] So, what should leaders do? The first is to stay in touch with them when they are gone. This can be formalized in an alumni network, so ask your HR department to set one up. Or it can be more informal, by giving them a call and sending them a note every once in a while. A few brave leaders have told me they actively help talent build their career by introducing them to people in their network, helping them plan next career steps. When you leave the door open, the chances are higher that talent will come back, with a rucksack full of knowledge and skills. I met an HR director of a multinational recently whose sole recruitment strategy was to re-hire people that once worked for the firm, as far back as twenty years ago. For her, this worked really well. The corporation already knew the people and vice versa. She said it felt like skipping the first two rounds of the interview process and mutually deep diving into a meaningful conversation about how they could be of benefit to each other.

STRATEGIC TAKEAWAY

Leaders should create a culture of appreciation and empathy. This way, personal relationships among employees will improve, which in turn will increase trust. Furthermore, invest in ties with ex-employees, e.g. through an alumni network.

Future Human Behavior

3.
The 'You Know Me' Society

3.1 Nothing on me
3.2 Digital James knows you
3.3 I know how you feel
3.4 Use my data! Fast forward to the past
3.5 Privacy paradox
3.6 My data, my € $ ¥ £
3.7 *Black Mirror* vs. Singularity University

INTRODUCTION

One spring morning I got into my car and fired up Google Maps – I am an avid user of the app. I was quite surprised to find the blue arrow that points in the direction of travel had been replaced by the image of a yellow van. Now our family car happens to be a... yellow van! Which is not the most common of cars. I had used Google Maps the evening before and although no one had fiddled with my phone to adjust something in the settings, the app magically gave me our yellow van. Although I loved this nifty feature, I also wondered: how does Google know we have a yellow van? I posted the question online. One smart commenter suggested that Google 'received' the information from a parking app I use. As that app knows our license plate, then it follows that they also know the make and color of our car.

This prompted me to question just how much 'they' do know about me and how much information about me is out there? And I am not alone in this. During the 2010s people began to realize their personal data was out there and slowly but steadily being used by various organizations. The beginning of the 21st century was a rat race, with organizations and governments harvesting as much people data as (legally and technically) possible. Sometimes with a clear goal behind it, but primarily just because they could. The more people data the better; getting it is easy, storing it is cheap and if we don't now, we'll figure out how to capitalize on it tomorrow! As an example, when I recently downloaded my Google data – and I consider myself a quite analog Gen X-er – I received 8.4GB of data: roughly 2 million Word documents. And that is just my Google data.

> Getting it is easy, storing it is cheap and if we don't now, we'll figure out how to capitalize on it tomorrow

What does the harvesting and use of this data mean for individuals and for society as a whole? Do people like this or do they find it creepy and suspicious?

If this trend continues, we will come to a point where all our information will be out there and when analyzed it would mean that a complete picture of our personality, needs, fears, dreams, hopes, secrets etc. could be created. What would this mean for society? For business? What would companies do if they knew everything about their customers? What would governments do if they knew everything about their citizens?

3.1

NOTHING ON ME

When discussing the rapid digitalization of society and the mass harvesting of data, I often encounter men – for some reason they are always men – who boast, "I am hardly on social media. They don't know anything about me!"

My response is always the same: "Well, actually they do."

There is no escaping public and private organizations collecting people data – except perhaps for those who decide to live as a hermit, in a Siberian cave. And even they might find a drone in front of their cave soon: "Say cheese!"

We share information and we gather information, which we share again. We do this continuously, both consciously and subconsciously, through websites, apps, digital assistants and smart devices. The vast majority of people are oblivious or just do not care about the many different technologies around them collecting their information. That nondescript weather app or that game for your daughter – downloaded for free – allows them to track your location and to collect and sell your data.

If you are now shrugging your shoulders, thinking, "I've got nothing to hide," then you are like most people.

Only a small percentage of people refuse to use mainstream social media or install certain apps because of privacy concerns. Some even brag with pride about being analog. But the fact of the matter is, although you can run, you cannot hide. For example, you too are on Facebook, because your network of friends, family and colleagues have put photos of you online – you at your neighborhood barbecue, your annual family ski trip or that conference you attended. Facebook scans the faces of everyone in these photos and creates so-called 'digital biometric templates'. It has been reported[1] that Facebook's facial recognition software – with the cool James Bond-ish name Deepface – is better than that of the FBI.

Who is this gentleman in the photo on the right? Easy answer, but how did you know? You cannot see his face and still you knew who it was through contextual analysis of his hair, ears, cheeks etc. Facebook is now capable of identifying you in pictures without seeing your face; it only needs your clothes, hair and body type to tag you in an image with 83% accuracy. The Chinese government's facial technology might be even better. In 2018, using their own facial recognition technology, they were already able to detect an individual criminal out of a crowd of 50,000 people in a stadium.

However, that is not all your network is doing. Many social media platforms ask users for permission to browse through their contact list: 'Find your friends!' Many people choose this easy option and allow social media platforms to use their entire contact list. With this, Facebook also saves contacts that are not on Facebook, thus creating so-called 'ghost profiles'. If your family members, friends, and colleagues all do the same, social media platforms can easily determine your name, contact information and your network, even if you do not use these platforms yourself. In other words, everyone's data is out there – even if you think you are the exception to the rule.

While the 2010s were about gathering data, the 2020s are defined by the follow-up question: how can this enormous pile of gathered data be used? And how should it be used, if at all? More information about each and every one of us is more easily available than ever before, to social media platforms, businesses, governments, and ourselves. Also, there is more and more software available to analyze this enormous amount of data, to help us find a job, a date, or a great book.

So where exactly is our data? Currently, it is scattered around in a variety of places: social media, search engines, data brokers like LiveRamp or Experian, app developers, IOT (Internet of Things), device makers, but also governments or hospitals. There is no central place, like a digital vault, where all the data is gathered and stored.

No one knows exactly what data is exactly where. What we do know is that our society is rapidly becoming more digitalized and an increasing amount of data is being generated, gathered, and analyzed. The vast majority of people simply have no idea just how much information on them is actually out there.

How do businesses possess so much information on their clients – us? The reason is that we have all been clicking, 'Yes, I agree' and 'Yes, I accept', to almost any terms and conditions and almost every service we use online. Whether booking a plane ticket online, buying a book on Amazon, using social media platforms, subscrib-

ing to an online newspaper or installing that fun game on your phone, you first have to accept the terms and conditions and agree to the privacy statement. We know that if we refuse to agree to the terms and conditions, the result will be no Facebook account and no plane ticket. In short, we are forced to click, 'I agree'. And after doing so for years and years most people now display so-called 'learned helplessness' behavior[2]. They have accepted their powerlessness and absence of control over the outcome of the situation and assume that control is not present.

Your biometric template and your ghost profile are out there

We click 'agree and accept' quite mindlessly. Over the past few years, several studies have examined what people do when asked to accept these terms & conditions. In all of these studies, the vast majority of people (between 70% and 99.9% – depending on the study), click yes, I agree. The brave minority that decide to review the terms and conditions have also been studied. They spend on average seven seconds looking at them.

What is the alternative? Only a fraction of the online products and services offer more expensive alternatives, where your privacy is protected, and your data is not stored and used. Paid messaging apps are out there, but with our entire social circle currently on free platforms like Facebook, WhatsApp, TikTok, Instagram, Snapchat, or WeChat, we are literally forced to use those apps, so as not to miss out socially. And those big players, whose business model it is to capitalize on the value of people data, will not stop collecting their clients' data anytime soon.

Everyone's data is out there —
even if you think you are the
exception to the rule

STRATEGIC TAKEAWAY

Instead of searching for value in the data you have – searching for the needle in a haystack – *turn the question around:* What data would you need for that new strategy or that wonderful innovation?

3.2

DIGITAL JAMES KNOWS YOU

Will there be better alternatives for protecting and disseminating your data in the future? Definitely. Let's take the rapid rise of AI powered digital assistants as an example. This is where we are now. Imagine hiring a real, live butler made of flesh and blood. Think of an old-fashioned British butler – we'll call him James. At the job interview, James has a surprising offer for you: "With regard to remuneration, you don't have to pay me. I will work for free. The only thing I ask in return, is that I be allowed to record some of the things you say and take some photos here and there. I might use that information to sell you some unique products and services that me and some acquaintances of mine also offer. I very much look forward to working with you!"

Would you hire this real-life, eavesdropping, photo-taking, information-sharing salesman-butler James? Most people would not. However, many people use digital assistants like Alexa, Siri, Google Assistant, and Cortana, which do the same as James proposes. These devices use your phone's microphone and increasingly your camera, to answer questions you have.

Not paying for these is like having a real human James running around your house with a microphone and a camera. I have shared this James dilemma with thousands of business professionals and students over the years and asked people if they'd be willing to pay a monthly subscription for a trustworthy privacy protected digital James. The vast majority would be more than happy to.

They could take their time, sit down, and spend a few hours training their digital assistant, just as they would a real human James. No one would employ a butler and have them guess how they would like their morning tea.[3] The digital James is not only a private help; many different business James's will soon be introduced. Again, we will train our business James, sit down regularly with him for a performance review, and so forth.

Getting back to today, the kind of people data out there is fairly comprehensive: location, network, contacts, shopping behavior, internet browsing history, personal information such as gender, age, nationality, ethnicity, educational background, relationship status, political and religious views, hobbies & interests, personal photos, call and text history, transaction history, all kinds of health information, and so forth.

The pile of people data is so large, that even if no new data were to be added, it would hardly matter. Most adults already have such a large digital footprint, it will be possible to analyze personality, preferences, and behavior for years to come.

How would you feel if
all AI suggestions were
perfect?

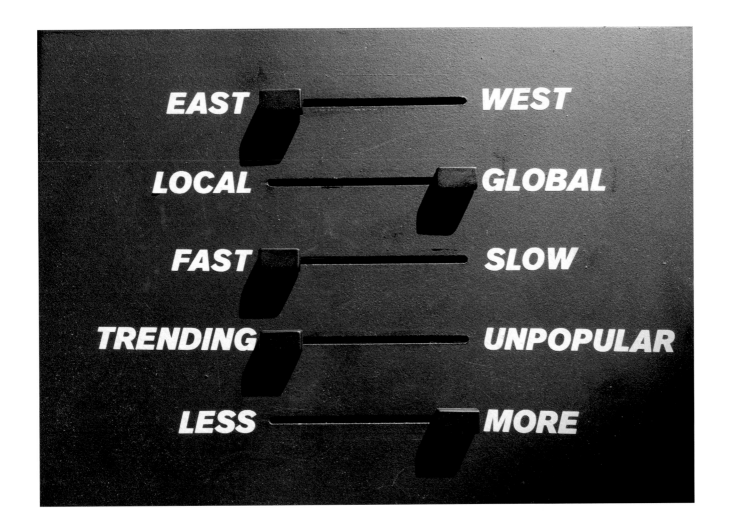

Most people would
freak out

So, what can businesses and governments do with our people data? Even today, it is fairly easy to create a personality profile by simply accessing the information people themselves have already put online, using social media. Most people assume that an accurate analysis, based on public social media information, is impossible, as people present a 'fake' perfect version of themselves online. But as far as psychologists are concerned, we can run but we can't hide.

We will pay and train our digital James

Algorithms don't need a lot of people data to accurately aggregate useful information. In a large study (over 86,000 participants), Stanford and Cambridge University examined the ability of computers versus people to make accurate judgments about personalities. The researchers created a piece of software that used Facebook likes to determine someone's personality and compared it to a personality self-assessment test, where people rated themselves using a standard academic, 100-item long questionnaire. The outcome was compared with the personality judgement of colleagues, friends, family members, and spouses of the participants. The results were staggering. By analyzing just 10 likes, researchers could more accurately predict a subject's personality than a co-worker; more than a friend or a roommate with 70 likes; a family member with 150 likes; and a spouse with 300 likes.

The researchers conclude, from the result of these studies, that we can also make computers emotionally intelligent in the near future. The researchers state, "AI [Artificial Intelligence] retains and accesses large quantities of information (...) while humans tend to focus on fewer data points and non-rational ways of thinking."[4]

There are commercial solutions which use the same kind of technology. Watson, IBM's supercomputer, is also applying its AI powers to the world of personality analysis. IBM sells its Personality AI as a service and the demo-mode, at the time of writing, is quite impressive; the personality analysis is elaborate and in-depth.[5] Another example is McKinsey's Afiniti algorithm. This is a contact center solution that matches up customers with support agents based on personality. In most cases that means a customer gets someone on the phone with a matching personality, set-up by using data gathered from Afiniti's clients, third parties, and company call history. As a result, McKinsey reports benefits like an improved customer experience, shorter handling times per call and therefore increased revenues.

If the AI of today can already create such accurate profiles, imagine what would happen if organizations were to start combining more data sets. The results would be staggering, with computers able to assess us better than our friends and family, even better than ourselves.

This last thought is worth exploring. As people, we want to feel like we make our own unique decisions. Werner Vogels, the CTO of Amazon, has disclosed in an interview that Amazon is able to predict to a high degree what people want when they visit Amazon's website. They tested this feature but decided not to roll it out; it scared customers and made them feel as though Amazon was 'in their head'. While they did actually want what Amazon was suggesting, they did not buy it. Consequently, the recommendation engine was turned back to its original 'imperfect' settings to show less of what it can actually do. Believing that our decisions are predictable, especially by a piece of software, is too unnerving.

This is most likely the reason the Netflix recommendation algorithm also gives 'bad' suggestions. How would you feel if all the suggestions were perfect? Most people would freak out. So, Netflix throws a few odd suggestions into the mix.[6] The result? People feel they are still in control of their own decisions.

How would you feel if all the suggestions were perfect? Most people would freak out

In showing people things they like and a few things they do not like, is it possible to achieve a perfect equilibrium? The answer is yes and no. There is no one-size-fits-all solution. There is a large group of people who love their own bubble and would not think of leaving the comfort of it. These people eat pasta every Friday, fish and chips every Sunday and go to the same campsite every summer. On the other side of the spectrum, there is a smaller group of people who cannot be pinned down on set preferences, constantly being on the lookout for new adventures and experiences. The vast majority of people, however, though they love their filter bubble, enjoy stepping out of it at times.

In the long run, we can expect to slowly get used to these types of technologies and gradually, we will allow them to decide more and more for us. Consuming pop culture is quite an easy one and I personally cannot go without my Spotify Discover Weekly list. But other applications are only a small step away. It is only a matter of time before technology can recommend the perfect job, the perfect politician or the perfect partner for us. The fact that many people don't like their job, their government officials or have a

hard time finding a spouse begs the question – why not have technology lend a helping hand? A member of the IBM Watson team told me: "We see IBM Watson as a calculator in the hands of a mathematician. It's not making decisions for them. It just helps a mathematician to be better at their job."

And yes, that is a lot of power for the algorithms and the tech firms behind them. Many people are concerned about this. With their predictive capabilities also comes an increased responsibility to use these capabilities ethically. More on the ethical side in Chapter 5.

STRATEGIC TAKEAWAY

Digital assistants are rapidly evolving and today they are free, but soon we will pay for them to be privacy protected. We will also see dedicated digital business assistants become available to the world of professionals. The idea of letting these assistants best-guess how they can help us will be short-lived: we will spend time with them, training them, and having performance reviews with them – almost as with a real human colleague.

3.3
I KNOW HOW YOU FEEL

Much of the technology around us is quite static: it responds to what we do – push a button, click on a link – but not to how we feel. That is about to change. The technology to assess someone's emotions is here and it works surprisingly well already. One of the key questions for the 2020s will be: what are we going to do with all the data of a person's real-time emotions? How do we protect privacy while still improving customer experience, making the world safer or hiring a more diverse work force?

Dozens of tech companies can already determine exactly how a person feels with the help of a camera and/or microphone. This technology is called 'Emotion AI'. It uses software to analyze visuals (face) and sound (voice) to determine one's emotions. In the late 2010s this technology could already outperform people in assessing human emotions correctly. More variables will be added in the future, which will make it even more accurate. Think of temperature and moisture sensors for example, to determine if people are getting nervous and starting to sweat.

The market leader in this field, Affectiva, claims that by analysing voice and facial expressions, they can measure the following human emotions with over 90% accuracy: anger, con-

tempt, disgust, engagement, fear, joy, sadness, surprise, and emotional valence. There are several studies which show that emotion AI is already outperforming humans in assessing emotions correctly.[7]

How is that possible? The main reason is that we over-estimate our own ability to assess facial expressions and body language accurately. We think we know how people really feel, but we don't. Imagine what would happen if people really could assess a fellow human being's true emotions and even expose white lies, instantly. It would fundamentally change all human interaction as white lies are part of our social fabric and can sometimes be of benefit in relationships.[8]

With the introduction of emotion AI, we are stepping into unknown territory – and this is not far into the future. It is here today.

Many companies, like Unilever, Delta Airlines, Hilton, and Vodafone use Emotion AI, which is developed by Hirevue, in their recruitment process. Applicants are asked to place themselves in front of their webcam and answer questions put to them by a piece of software. The software analyzes both what candidates say and how they say it. Are they happy, sad, confident, nervous…? The software can also give

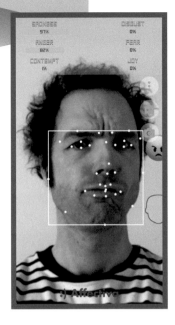

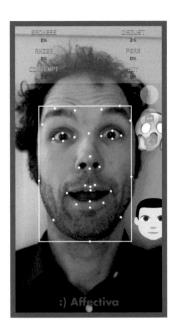

Emotion AI gives an honesty rating to your interview answers

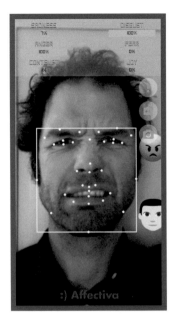

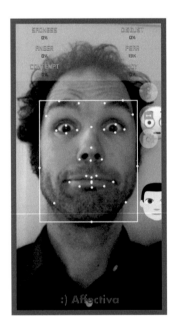

an 'honesty rating' to the answers of the candidates. Some vendors give this feature a cool name like 'Credibility Assessment Technology', which might sound very futuristic, but in fact is the 21st century version of the polygraph. The company Converus claims an 86% accuracy rate in detecting a lie by analyzing subtle changes in the subject's eyes. Border security around the world is running pilots using emotion AI at border crossings.

Many car manufacturers offer a 'driver drowsiness detection' system in their new cars. With a camera or other sensors in the dashboard, the car detects if a driver is getting tired and can 'wake up' the driver, using vibration in the steering wheel or an audio signal. This technology is really useful, as 20% of car accidents are estimated to be fatigue-related. If this technology is developed further, AI can make for an easy transition to the self-driving car, where the AI monitors the driver and can assist when necessary.

The company Shelfpoint creates smart supermarket shelves with built-in LED screens and micro cameras that are able to detect shoppers' emotions. If a shopper is interested in buying a specific product, an LED screen will provide extra, customizable information about the product, a special offer or anything that will drive a 'buy' decision. Shelfpoint claims to boost sales to double digit growth compared to the standard shelves as we know them. For example, if I wanted to know more about the nutritional value of a product, the LED screens would automatically present me with that information.

The latter example has been given a warm welcome by my retail and sales clients, but most other audiences respond with screams of outrage. My advice would be to not roll this out tomorrow as people do not want this – yet.

An absolutely wonderful example is that of Barcelona Comedy Club Teatreneu. It tested a business model using emotion AI, where audi-

ence members enter free of charge to a comedy show. In front of every audience seat is a camera filming the face of the person sitting there. The theater has emotion AI software running, so it can track the emotions of all individual audience members. Now this is a comedy club, so people will laugh, but when they do they start paying! Every laugh will cost €0.30 with a cap of €24, so punters go home cheerful, not broke. People can track their laughter score on individual screens placed on each seat. It will be a while yet, but I am waiting for Netflix to launch a similar feature.

Ethical question: do we want this technology to 'tell' us how others are feeling?

Emotion AI could also be used when we are listening to music, watching a movie or playing a video game. Media companies constantly want to know how their users are feeling. They will be able to adapt their product to match the emotion of a person or group of people – in real time. An early 'real time' example is the computer game Nevermind, which uses Affectiva's emotion AI. The gameplay is adjusted, based on the user's level of fear.

What's next for emotion AI? Expectations are huge. Emotion AI, also called the affective computing market, is estimated to become a billion-dollar market in the mid-2020s.[9] The business opportunities seem endless.

During Covid, Affectiva released a test video in which the participants were in a Zoom call (all Affective employees) and their emotions were analyzed in real-time. The only parameter that was switched for this demo was 'group valence'

What happens if we
outsource part of our
EQ to emotion AI?

(an overall measure of how positive/negative an experience is). Imagine as a leader having the full dashboard switched on for your next Zoom or Teams meeting. Just being able to see the group's attention or engagement in real-time would most likely lead to quite a few adjustments to any meeting.

People will be able to analyze the emotions of the person on the other side of the table. If it's currently working in digital job interviews and telephone helpdesks, it is only a small step to use this technology in a real physical conversation; for example a date, a business negotiation, or a courtroom.

Emotion AI will be used as a tool to improve our own physical and mental well-being and that of others, from leaders wanting to know how their people are doing, to parents who would like to know how their silent 14-year-old adolescent is feeling. From a technical perspective it will be possible to monitor and help people with emotional or mental issues, in real time.

However, there is then an ethical question: do we want this technology to 'tell' us how others are feeling?

We are used to trusting our own inner emotional dashboard to determine how people around us are feeling. But what happens if we outsource part of our EQ to emotion AI – an emotion calculator? If we look at the research into the effects of the mathematical calculator for comparison, we can see two things: there is no evidence we've gotten worse at (mental) math and when used well, calculators can boost math skills.[10] Using this analogy, we need to find ways to use emotion AI well, so we will be able to appropriately boost our EQ.

Since governments and businesses want to use these types of technologies, their widespread presence in the future will be unavoidable. In China, behavior on and offline is con-

stantly being monitored to determine if it's socially acceptable – what if emotion AI technology is added as well? If you want to apply for a job in Unilever today, you have to pass their emotion AI algorithm. Some business conferences monitor the emotions of the audience, to give the organizers real time feedback.

As emotion AI further develops, its usage will stimulate more public debate and it will be hedged around by new legislation. The questions we can already start answering today are the fundamental ones: what are we going to do with this technology as a society, a government, a business, as individuals? When is it beneficial and when is it harmful? There is a whole chapter on the Future of Ethics, where we'll deep dive into this question.

STRATEGIC TAKEAWAY

Emotion AI will be one of the big technologies of the 2020s and beyond. Leaders will have to ask themselves if, in fact, they really want to instantly measure the emotions of their applicants, their people, their customers. This data might turn a current business strategy upside down, but should you? Is it in line with your business and personal values?

EXERCISE

HOW DO YOU FEEL ABOUT EMOTION AI?

We are used to digitally sharing our location, search history, shopping preferences, network and vacation photos, and much more. But are we ready to share our emotions as well? For this exercise, please have one person explain the following case study of Unilever & Hirevue to a group of people.

CASE: UNILEVER & HIREVUE

Unilever was one of the first multinationals to use emotion AI, having outsourced the initial part of their application process to this technology. More specifically, candidates were required to pass three algorithms before being invited to the Unilever office and meet a real person. Algorithm #1 analyses a candidate's resume or LinkedIn profile without needing a cover letter; algorithm #2 determines if candidates are really as smart as their resumes and profiles claim, by having them play neuroscience-based games; and lastly, algorithm #3 is comprised of a video interview, but not with a real person. Instead, a computer program will ask the questions, while the emotion AI software scans the candidate's emotions during the job interview.

After a year of testing these algorithms globally, Unilever reported that this method was very successful. The number of applications doubled and it reduced the hiring process time from four months to four weeks. But most interestingly, Unilever claimed that the process resulted in hiring its most diverse group of new Unilever employees ever. It programmed the algorithm to be diverse in gender, ethnicity and socio-economic backgrounds.

This means that the old way of hiring, by human Unilever HR professionals, led to a less diverse group of employees. Although not directly argued by Unilever, between the lines it can be read that the HR AI is morally 'better' than their own

people. This might sound strange, but it is not. For decades it has been known that people hiring people is a very subjective process and that individuals have a strong tendency to hire people like themselves.

Ask the group to discuss the case in pairs. Two questions can be asked:

1. What do you think of this technology in general?
2. If your company were to use this technology for recruiting new candidates, how would you program it?

After a set time for discussion in pairs, ask the group this question: how do you feel about emotion AI? Please provide the following three options for an answer:

1. It's great, I see many positives for the world and my organization!
2. Hmm, I see the good and the bad. We need to weigh these two sides and then proceed with caution.
3. No way! This is end of the world technology. I mainly see the negative aspects of this.

Have the group raise their hands and see how many people are a 1, 2, or 3.

The last step is a group discussion. In my experience, every group has number 1's and 3's. To get a lively debate going, have the number 1's and 3's explain their points of view.

3.4

USE MY DATA! FAST FORWARD TO THE PAST

From a historical perspective, the developments discussed in this chapter are not all that new. We return to the world, as it was before the 20th century, where almost everything was custom-made as there was little to no mass production. People got their groceries in local stores where they knew the owner and the employees. If you needed a closet, a carpenter would build one for you – that was the only option.

Mass-production in the 20th century has dehumanized integral parts of the consumer experience. We all sit on similar mass-produced chairs, wear the same sneakers that are available everywhere and eat food which is made to taste globally the same. When it comes to customer support we are being increasingly transferred to a helpdesk (in a different country) where agents work for several different clients.

With the right use of data however, we can enter an era of mass humanisation. Where technology could refashion the world around us into a more individual experience. A world where organizations know us so well they can customize and personalize products and experiences, to the same level as a small local grocer could in 1900. It would actually mean we would go back

to how life once was: where companies knew their clients and politicians knew their citizens and vice versa. We should not be surprised that people crave to be known, to be acknowledged, to be treated as someone special, instead of just a number.

I will give you the permission you need to make more use of my data

A slow but fundamental shift in society is taking place, as people increasingly realize that their data, if used well by organizations, can make life better. As an example, I have worked extensively for a large multinational telecommunications company. Together with a group of experts, we organized a series of workshops called 'the future of the customer experience' around the globe. These workshops were partially composed of consumer and corporate clients participating in focus groups on this topic.

Mass-production in the 20th century has dehumanized integral parts of the consumer experience

The most interesting insight was that customers said: "Dear telco, you know me!" Meaning: I've been a client for years, you have my data, it's a digital world, so treat me as special! Some customers asked: "Why are you still treating me like a number?" People from the telco replied to the customers by telling them about the legal restrictions governing their use of personal data. To which customers replied: "I trust you. I will give you the permission you need to make more use of my data."

It is a slow shift in mindset. Many of my clients report a growing irritation amongst their customers if their data is not being used to provide them with a tailored, personal customer experience – "I get special treatment with the Amazons and Netflixes of this world, why can't you give me that as well?" The shift is fundamental: if I trust you, then please use my data.

STRATEGIC TAKEAWAY

Organizations should ask themselves how they can humanize their products and services by using people data. For larger organizations not to do this means little or no humanization and that will increasingly prove to be a problem as people are getting used to their data being used well by organizations they trust.

3.5

PRIVACY PARADOX

The fact that people increasingly expect their data to be used does not mean that all data can be used by every organization for any purpose. A relationship based on trust is crucial, privacy is increasingly important – and young people are most aware of this.

The latter is interesting, as many experts thought each generation would become a bit more open than the previous one. Marc Zuckerberg once famously said, in an interview about privacy, that social norms had changed and that the age of privacy was over.[12] With Generation Z the tide has turned. Research shows they care about their privacy and are more aware of their digital vulnerability than older generations.[13] [14] They have a growing data awareness and are actually increasingly algorithm aware. Students have said to me: "I won't google that, because then Google will think it's of interest to me!"

I have got nothing to hide!

Research into general attitudes towards privacy show that the vast majority of people claim that privacy is important to them. In actual practice however, hardly anyone takes concrete measures to protect their privacy. This is a classic example of an intention-behavior gap (also known as the value-action gap). People consider privacy to be important, and research confirms their desire and intention to protect it, but in fact, people's actual behavior indicates the opposite. In other words, there is a gap between what people say and what people do. This gap is so profound that researchers have named it 'the privacy paradox'.[15]

In several studies on privacy, researchers have asked respondents if they would be willing to pay for their social media profiles, navigation software, and games, and to have their privacy protected in return. Again, the majority of people respond that they do not want to pay for these services.[16] Their reasoning for that, and I have heard this in workshops too many times to count, is what I call the 'I have got nothing to hide!' fallacy. A statement always met with nods of agreement by the other participants. And yes, it's a psychological hurdle to start paying for something that used to be free. But as we become more aware that, 'if you are not paying for the product, you are the product', attitudes to privacy will change. It is expected that we will see more paid – privacy protected – versions of free digital products and services become available. However, paying for privacy protection means it will be bought by those who can afford it. The ethical dilemma and the underlying question for society remains: is privacy a human right or a luxury product?

The challenge with privacy is that it's an intangible good. It will only be missed when it's gone. Most of us believe that guarding our privacy is the responsibility of government: 'They should protect us!' However, if the government is overly protective, people get irritated; look at the response to the widely criticized EU cookie

law. And if people experience their data being used in a beneficial way, for example the recommendation algorithm of Netflix and Spotify, there is no way back. We do not want to manually browse through thousands of movies and television series yet again to find that gem.

The 2010s was a decade of a number of data hacks and privacy scandals. From the online theft of millions of credit cards, to leaked nude celebrity photos, and from smart viruses (like WannaCry) to the data breach of Cambridge Analytica. For some, these have been profound warning signs, but to the majority of the population they have not been the wake-up call that could make them change their behavior and turn away from the Facebooks of this world.

In the 2010s, China introduced the Social Credit System, which monitors citizens, behavior online, while cameras and microphones monitor them on the streets. Good behavior is rewarded, and bad behavior is punished. For example, if you run a red pedestrian light, cameras with facial recognition will note that and your Citizen Score will decrease. On the other hand, you can raise your score if you publish positively about the government online. This is the principle of gamification applied to citizenship, but the consequences on people's daily lives are very real. A person's Credit Score will affect their internet speed, access to certain restaurants and leisure facilities or freedom to travel abroad. Additionally, one's Credit Score determines insurance premiums, social security benefits, or eligibility to get a loan.

The response from people in Western countries when hearing about this system is one of shock, fear, and apocalyptic doom scenarios. This is Big Brother 2.0, where everything you do is monitored and evaluated and privacy has moved from being a human right to a government's right – a right to know (and to some extent control) you. In China however, people respond to this social credit system with nonchalance; foreign journalists raise concerns. The problem here of course is that if you ask those who live in a surveillance society about that very surveillance society, you are very unlikely to receive credible answers.

If you are not paying for the product, you are the product

In Western countries, we have a few similar systems in place. For example, in the Netherlands, I currently receive an 80% discount on my car insurance premium because of my 'good driving behavior'. Meaning that I have never damaged my car. Now I am thinking of switching to an insurance firm that logs the way I drive with a digital tracker; if I drive safely, I get an even higher discount. Speaking of cars, Dutch highways are packed with speed cameras filming all cars. Only speeding cars get fined. European football stadiums are packed with smart cameras, which can detect violent behavior, but also pick up racial slurs with speech recognition technology.

The big difference is that China has more monitoring systems than Europe and combines all of these into one overall 'score'. The workings of the Chinese algorithms are also classified, so there is little transparency around how the system actually works.

Another country that has gone fully digital is Estonia. They were the forerunners, creating digital citizenship in the 1990s – earning the nickname E-Stonia. Everything in the country is, and

can be, done digitally, from taxes to healthcare to starting a company. Estonians have complete control over their personal data. Citizens have access to a portal where they can see a log of every organization that has accessed their personal data. If citizens feel that an organization has wrongfully accessed their data, they can report it to an ombudsman. A civil servant will then examine the case to decide whether the practice was justified or not.

Safety is one of the reasons the country decided to 'go digital' on such a scale. In the case of occupation, say by Russia, Estonia's businesses, property ownership, citizenship, etc. is safely stored in the Cloud. When the occupation is over, the whole country can be restored from the back-up with one click of a button. Many foreign analysts are concerned that such a system is vulnerable to abuse by the Estonian government. Can the Estonians trust their government to treat their data responsibly? A former prime minister of Estonia is famous for his response to that question: Stalin didn't need any digital technology to massacre 20 million people and if you want to do harm, you will, one way or the other.

STRATEGIC TAKEAWAY

Organizations have to walk a fine line between protecting people's data and using it. Concerns about privacy are on the increase and this trend will continue as young people – Generation Z – are very keen on protecting their privacy.

3.6

MY DATA, MY € $ ¥ £

People are slowly realizing that their data can be used to their advantage and disadvantage, and that it is an incredibly valuable asset. In an ideal world, people would have all their own data in a digital safe and would be able to control which organizations and individuals are allowed to access which parts of their personal data. We would be in control of deciding which data to disclose for free, or in return for a (monetary) incentive.

Since this requires a lot of time and effort, there are a number of companies trying to play a trustworthy, middleman, data broker role. These are all new, 'start-uppy' and relatively small. Companies like Wibson, Datum, CitizenMe, Ocean Protocol, and Datacoup, offer rewards for sharing personal data. For now, these companies only offer tiny amounts in exchange for your personal data: a few cents here, a few cents there. Potentially, this could be a huge new line of business, their size and impact possibly comparable to search engines and social media companies.

In the 2020s we will see more initiatives to try and give individuals back control of their data, while taking a percentage of a people data exchange. Apple has already introduced 'Privacy as a Service', which is a start. But it probably won't be the traditional players, like Alphabet or Facebook, that will make this into more than just a service. After all, it goes directly against their business models. Maybe we should let Estonia run with this one?

It is important to note that not all data is of equal worth. The personal data of high-income people, or couples who are about to buy a home, will be worth more to data brokers than the data from a poor, unemployed senior, living on welfare. And this could create new inequalities; my data is worth more than your data.

The seat belt was made mandatory more than 100 years after its invention

If we get a system like this to work, it would be as a fair exchange. Data brokers might share our health data with our trusted supermarket for example, so we are advised to buy foods that will improve our health or help us run that marathon in under three hours. Data brokers could utilise education data to help students discover an ideal course of study or find their future dream job. Our travel history and interests would help us to find that gem of a hidden holiday spot, one that we'll both love and can afford.

But first, we will have to experiment to see what works and what does not, as with any other form of innovation. This will result in successes and failures. We can expect plenty of people data breaches or social credit systems going haywire. But we will have to be patient. Take the car industry. It took them 70 years after the first automobile was produced to make the seat belt mandatory for all cars. Millions of people had already died in crashes up until that point (in the US alone there were 4 million deaths). Surprisingly, the seat belt was not a new invention. It was invented and patented before the first car was ever built, in the mid-1800s. So, let's have the privacy discussion now and not wait until 2100.

STRATEGIC TAKEAWAY

Organizations will have to realize that increasingly, people want something back for their data and ideally as a fair exchange. This might disrupt quite a few business models. Also, think about a future where people outsource their personal data to a data broker, who will negotiate on their behalf.

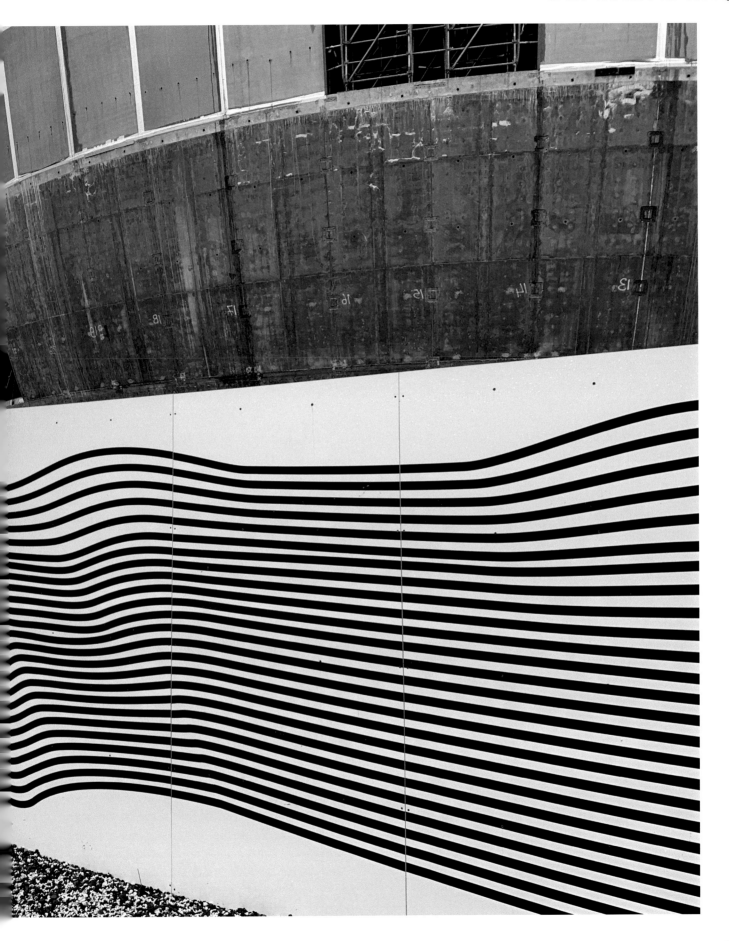

3.7

BLACK MIRROR VS. SINGULARITY UNIVERSITY

Many of the technologies and possible futures discussed in this chapter are reflected in the famous Channel 4 and Netflix series *Black Mirror*, a dystopian science fiction show set in the near future. In most episodes, the unanticipated negative consequences of current technology are explored, tapping deep into the human fear that technology will destroy the world. *Black Mirror* has become a cultural reference point comparable to 1984, *Minority Report* and HAL9000 in Kubrick's *2001: A Space Odyssey*. Many episodes of *Black Mirror* feel so real, it affects our thinking about current and new technologies and decision making.

Popular culture influences the way we think about real world events and our memory of historic events is influenced by the fiction we have consumed. How many hours has the average American adult spent watching Western movies compared to the amount of hour spent studying the same historic era in high school? And which was the more compelling and memorable? The same principle applies to thinking about the future: how much time does the average person spend deliberately thinking about and discussing the implications of future technologies – preferably based on research and not gut feeling? Our thinking on future technology has been influenced by shows like *Black Mirror*. In every episode, future tech has a spectacularly negative implication for society and human behavior. This is fiction of course, but I have witnessed it influencing quite a few boardroom discussions.

There are polar opposites. For example the Singularity University, which has gathered a lot of fans in boardrooms as well. This think tank, co-founded by futurist Ray Kurzweil, believes that if we reach the point of singularity (when computers surpass all human intelligence by a billion-fold, estimated to happen in 2045), we will see a computer intelligence explosion. Then, technology will provide solutions for the global crises that humans are facing today, such as energy and food shortages, and cures for an array of terminal or impacting illnesses. This is a very attractive narrative *and* rooted in research. It is a wonderful, positive mindset for brainstorming the endless opportunities offered by technology.

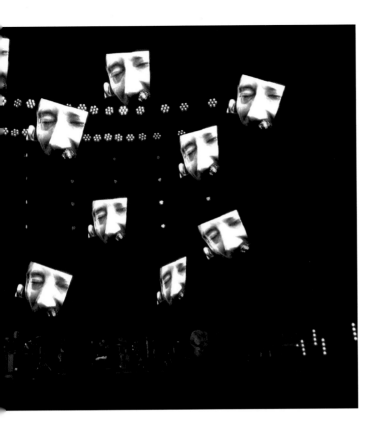

Watch a *Black Mirror* episode and a Singularity University keynote in one go

As with most things in life, the truth is found somewhere in the middle. *Black Mirror* raises valid concerns – like the famous episode, *Nosedive* – where every human and every human interaction is rated – and we will see some of these scenarios play out in some form in real life. In recent years, there have been a number of privacy breaches, that have seriously impacted people's lives. The same goes for the Singularity University solutions: there are several algorithms assisting medical professionals in the diagnostic process, and some of these are already outperforming human diagnoses.[17]

Both are sides of the same coin, and both are valid in a boardroom discussion about new and future technology. It's hard though, not to fall for the black and white thinking fallacy. Even quality news media serves us these two narratives to sensationalize our possible futures; experts who employ black or white thinking make for a more provocative interview, rather than balanced experts who predict a gray future. This future might be more complicated, diffuse, and to some, boring. But it is the most likely scenario.

Rather than being riled by the TED talk where a futurist explains that AI will save the world, future-proof leaders will need to create some balance in their thinking, by watching a *Black Mirror* episode. Both perspectives are needed, as they are two sides of the same coin.

STRATEGIC TAKEAWAY

When discussing or adopting new technology prepare yourself and your people for the good and the bad, as that is what it is. Using new technology always has unforeseen consequences, so anticipate and embrace these early on.

4.
Digital Balance

4.1 *Hate:* from technophobia to algorithm aversion
4.2 *Love:* digital addiction
4.3 Phubbing – ignoring people
4.4 The Future: counter trend, digital butlers & apathy
4.5 Digital balance as a luxury
4.6 Practicing patience in a world that's speeding up
4.7 The future of human work

INTRODUCTION

When I meet new people and tell them what I do, I am often bombarded with questions about the future. The most popular question is *"How do I strike a sane digital balance?"* This question comes in a variety of forms.

In business the question revolves around how digital or physical a customer experience or recruitment strategy should be and what the ideal balance between working from home versus office work is. There are also questions on the future use of algorithms versus human workers – "Is technology going to replace us?" Indeed, questions around striking a digital balance can apply to almost any part of business.

Outside the business world, questions may come from parents who are looking for a digital balance in their homes and wonder how much technology they should allow/recommend to their children. A lot of people complain about their life partner being glued to a screen and what to do about it. I also have students who admit they will only go on a date after a digital match from a platform like Tinder and do not dare to strike up an impromptu, real conversation in a bar.

How digital will our lives get? How digital will
society get? And how will that impact our
behavior?

As explained in 1.7, the extremes of a black and
white narrative in answer to these questions – the
fully digital or fully disconnected future – are most
entertaining, and tend to feature prominently in the
media, on social media, and in popular culture.

How digital are we getting, what is the perfect balance?

But reality is more often grayscale. Society will
find a – fragile and dynamic – digital balance
where we will continue to combine the best of the
technological/digital with the best of the physical/
human. It will be a rollercoaster ride getting there,
but the sooner we accept that this dynamic digital
balance is our light at the end of the tunnel, the
sooner we'll get there.

4.1

HATE: FROM TECHNOPHOBIA TO ALGORITHM AVERSION

People have a deeply ambivalent relationship with new technology. Any new technology is met with a dualistic response. We love it, we hate it, we want it, we don't want it, we can't manage without it, and we are afraid of it. Most people experience a combination of these feelings, all at the same time.

Let's look at the negative reaction to new technology. This response has been thoroughly documented and well-researched throughout history. Many forms of new technology have been met with this negative response, from a small percentage of people to, sometimes, the majority of society.[1] It has been described as technophobia, technopanic, automation anxiety, or – and this is my current favorite - 'algorithm aversion'.[2] The latter refers to people who dislike and distrust the algorithms that make decisions for humans.

In the introduction to this book, I describe the reluctance of people to board the automatic elevator in 1900. There are dozens of other great historic examples that show us how technology might change, but people's responses don't.

In the 16th century, people responded the same way to the printing press as we do today to artificial intelligence. They believed the printing press would lead to an information overload that would be "confusing and harmful to the mind."[3] Furthermore, it would put monks, who copied books by hand, out of work, which would in turn "destroy their souls."[4] In the 18th century, when books were widely available, many experts concluded that "the free access which many young people have to romances, novels, and plays has poisoned the mind and corrupted the morals of many a promising youth and prevented others from improving their minds in useful knowledge." [5] Was this a new line of thought? No, it was old news. More than two millennia ago, Socrates famously warned parents against writing as it would "create forgetfulness in the learner's soul, because they will not use their memory."[6] Two millennia later Socrates was proven wrong. Writing something down by hand is actually the best way to remember it.[7]

A more recent example is the introduction of the radio. In the 1920s and 1930s so many people were afraid of the harmful effect of radio

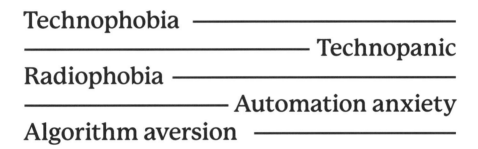

Technophobia ————————————————

———————————————— Technopanic

Radiophobia ————————————————

———————————————— Automation anxiety

Algorithm aversion ————————————————

waves and loudspeakers, 'radiophobia' became a household term.[8] And as with any new technology, the radio would harm our youth the most, distract young people in education and impair their performance in school. It was reported that children had "developed the habit of dividing attention between the preparation of their school assignments and the compelling excitement of the loudspeaker."[9]

This kind of reasoning sounds all too familiar. It's caused by our (in)famous negativity bias; the human tendency to focus on the negative. Indeed, the introduction of new technologies like the radio or the television were very exciting and might have influenced a few youngsters' school results, but on average, school scores

and intelligence levels went up throughout the 20th century.[10]

So, is there any truth in the worries of the so-called technophobes? Yes and no. We might wish a new technology to always be positive and only improve our lives, but unfortunately every good seems to come with some bad as well. The question is, can we accept a dualistic outcome?

Let's use the car in a simple thought exercise. Yes, the car has given us mobility, freedom to travel and vastly boosted the global economy, but it also causes more than one million deaths a year globally.[11] That's more than all wars and homicides combined, a staggering figure. Imagine if we could go back to the year 1900. If we had known then that the car would end up killing over a million people a year globally, would we have allowed it on the road and continued its development? It didn't take long for cars to turn very deadly. Vehicle-related deaths are currently at the same level as they were in the 1930s.[12]

Would we have allowed the automobile to be developed if we had known it would kill a million people annually?

One million people getting killed each year seems to be a mere statistic to the media in comparison to the hype surrounding the few fatal accidents there have been so far with Teslas, or self-driving Ubers. The current debate suggests that this whole development must be stopped, because one death would be one too many. This is a valid point, but what about the other side of the coin? How many deaths has the Tesla autopilot already prevented? Can it be measured? Probably not with the small numbers of those type of cars on the road today.

So, we can try to keep the bad side of technology to a minimum, but we can't make it disappear. Can we accept that the bad comes with the good, or that at least a little bad, comes with the good? Are we shifting to a society where even a little bad is too much? And what does this mean for the advancement of new technology? In the Apollo space program, 17 astronauts died before the successful moon landing mission. Would we accept a similar sacrifice today when it comes to new technology?

I am afraid not. The self-driving car promises to save a million lives a year, but society seems to be unwilling to accept that it will make mistakes too and could cause fatalities. We want technology to be perfect, instantly.

How can we make sure all this new technology will have a smooth landing in society? I truly believe organizations and their leaders should let go of the extreme negative and positive narrative and shift to the middle; new technology brings good and bad. I think a wonderful start would be tech CEOs stepping in and openly admitting this fact. Why did it take Mark Zuckerberg fifteen years to come to his senses and drop his Facebook-brings-only-great-things-to-everybody narrative? It would be better if the Zuckerbergs of the world were brave enough to say; "We have this radically new technology here. As it's so new, we do not really know what the impact of it on society will be. We embrace an open debate with experts, politicians and the general public on how we can make our technology work most effectively for the benefit of all." If you know of such a CEO, please let me know and they will be featured in all my keynotes.

STRATEGIC TAKEAWAY

Leaders have to accept and embrace the negative sides of new technology. This ranges from adapting to negative 'technophobic' responses from consumers and employees, to being open about (potential) negative outcomes and taking responsibility early on to minimize these.

4.2
LOVE: DIGITAL ADDICTION

Let's now deep dive into the 'love' side of new technology. With any new technology, there are a minority of people who immediately get very excited about it. These are often referred to as the 'early-adopters'. This group consists of people whofocus on the benefits of the new technology and simply want to try it out for themselves so they can decide if it's beneficial to them. This group is estimated to be around 13.5% of the population.[13] Everyone else will take their time to see if they like a technology and will jump on board later. Once a new technology gets adopted by the majority of people, it will find its place in society. Yet our acceptance of a new technology does not mean we all love it.

The 21st century saw a new kind of love for a new technology – our love for our smartphone. It's unlike anything we've experienced before. Yes, throughout history, people have loved the radio, the car, the television and the gaming console, but the smartphone is in a category of its own. Something completely different and not in one way, but in three ways.

Firstly: It is not a single piece of new technology, it is an all-in-one device.

Phone / Camera / Video camera / Television / Radio / Music player / Web browser / Navigation system / E-reader / Newspaper / Watch / Flashlight / Gaming console / Calculator

And it's rapidly becoming an unlimited access device with access to:

All the music / All the radio stations / All podcasts / All news papers / All books / All television shows / All movies / All games / And all information and all people

We have an archive of our culture and our history in our hands; access to anyone, anywhere. This is unprecedented and mind-blowing, and more features are being added constantly. Smartphones are getting more and more reliable health monitoring features and we are only just seeing the first glimpses of the AI-powered digital assistant features.

Secondly: All this is portable. People can take it everywhere with them, to the toilet, to bed. The newest generation of smartphones are waterproof. I have quite a few parents complain to me that their teenagers are taking their smartphones into the shower with them. And no, this is not a joke. To many people the smartphone feels like an extension of their body although it is not physically connected – yet.

Thirdly: It's social. Most researchers see the social layer as the most addictive element of the smartphone.[14] Keep in mind that social is not just social media. It's the social layer that's added almost everywhere: to the games we play, the videos we watch (YouTube) or the bike rides we go on (Strava). People are social creatures, and we crave connection. Without human connec-

The smartphone has super charged our social behavior

tion, life is less pleasurable – some would argue, meaningless. For example, let's go back half a century when a teenager bought a new record. What would they do the next day at school? Tell their friends all about it and invite them over to listen to the new record. The smartphone has super charged our social behavior. Imagine stumbling onto a brilliant video on YouTube. What is the first thing you do? Exactly. You share it. A shared experience is much more valuable than something experienced just by yourself.

This social layer is also a personal, real-time feedback machine. We crave the micro-feedback we get about ourselves. Whether it is a post on YouTube, WhatsApp or Instagram, a high score we achieved, or a bike ride we've completed, we love to see people responding to that. From a view to a like and from a share to a comment, these are all signs that what we've done matters to others and that we are being recognized and seen. The smartphone is a feedback machine confirming that we matter.

The smartphone is a new paradigm, a new category, it is such an all-encompassing technology, that not to get addicted is the exception.

Because yes, we are addicted. The research is abundant and conclusive, we have become literally addicted to our digital devices. A recent study found that people were already touching their phones almost a million times per year. And yes, that's an average.[15] The constant micro-rewards the smartphone gives tap into our dopamine system and the shots of dopamine we get with each view, comment, heart, response, or share are highly addictive. It is for that reason, researchers compare our smartphone use to an actual drug addiction, like cocaine. Medical professor Robert H. Lustig states that the smartphone is "not a drug, but it might as well be. It works the same way. It has the same results."

The brain gets used to high dopamine levels very quickly and if we don't get our regular social shots, we get stressed and suffer psychological and physical withdrawal symptoms. In several studies around the world, people have been asked not to use their devices for a few hours or even a few days. The vast majority of participants in these studies reflect the behaviors of real drug addicts when not getting their drugs. They get nervous and anxious, feel on the brink of a panic attack, start sweating, and their heart rate and blood pressure both go up. They also feel naked and experience a sense of loss or lessening of their extended self.[16][17]

It is a designer's job to make us love their creation

It's the social aspect that creates the most stress – the buzz term 'fear of missing out' (FOMO). The psychological principle of the FOMO is a ubiquitous one. Imagine a birthday party that all your friends are going to, but you can't make it. Of course, you will be wondering how the party is going and what you are missing out on. The smartphone ensures the party is going on all the time across multiple apps and platforms. FOMO is the reason you check your phone immediately when you wake up, during dinner and before you go to bed. The majority of people have experienced, or are experiencing, maybe even as we speak, ghost messages. These are the messages perceived to be coming in on your devices that are not coming in. People think their mobile phone is buzzing in their pocket, but it's not. Our brain is tricking us. By the way, have you recently checked your phone? Maybe you should. There might be a message waiting.

Consumers, experts and politicians tend to blame the tech companies, complaining that their software is designed to drive addiction.

This complaint is a futile one, as that is what designers are hired to do. Netflix series are constructed in such a way to keep us coming back for more. Our cars are designed to be as comfortable as possible, with air conditioning, superb stereos, comfortable seats, and every kind of gadget that you can imagine. Restaurants and bars are designed to give us a better experience than we have at home, so we keep coming back rather than staying in.

Yes, our personal tech devices will get even more features, and more importantly they will get to know us better and better. They will adapt to our emotions and with AR/VR and the next wave of digital assistants the lines between the physical and the virtual will blur more and more. This means people will potentially become ever more addicted to their devices in the coming years.

STRATEGIC TAKEAWAY

New technologies are only embraced, initially, by a small minority. But even when a technology gets picked up and is embedded in society, it doesn't mean people like or love it. The love for our smartphones cannot be compared to the love we have for other technologies – it is in a new category of its own.

How can I get a sane digital balance in my personal and my professional life?

EXERCISE

HOW ADDICTED ARE YOU?

In my workshops and keynotes, I often do a fun exercise where I ask the audience: "How addicted are you to your device(s)? Which can include a smartphone, tablet, laptop etc." Then I give people three options to choose from:

1.   I'm not addicted at all. I do have a smartphone but I haven't really thought about it in the past hour.

2.   Yes, ok, I am addicted but I'm in control.

3.   I need help. I need some therapy. Now.

Over the past few years, I have done this exercise with hundreds of groups of professionals and students all over the world, and surprisingly, the result is always roughly the same. About 10% of the audience can be categorized in the first group. They are totally happy with their device usage; they see themselves as not addicted at all. Then group 2, which makes up around 70%, admit they are addicted but it's under control. The last group is a steady 20% and these are the people who will, amongst a group of colleagues, stakeholders, partners, peers, etc. ad-mit they need help with their addiction. It also doesn't really matter if the core of the group is old or young, and this is important. Many of the executives I work with are a bit older, like myself – over 40 – and they think that the younger generation, the ones that grew up with digital technology, are fine and in control with *anything* digital. A bit like fish that don't know they're in the water as it's natural for them. Yet I have done this exercise with teenagers, students and young professionals around the world, and the results are similar everywhere.

One in three youngsters
admit they need help with
their digital addiction

There is a growing body of evidence in academic literature that supports the above. Yes, the majority of people, whether they are young or old, are fine with their devices and can 'manage' their addiction. But there is quite a large minority, in most studies it's between 25% and 40% of people, reporting to researchers that they are suffering from addiction to their devices.[18] What are the impacts for those in group 3? I've been asking this and the responses are always the same, whether it's students or senior executives:

"I'm constantly distracted. I can't concentrate."
"It's interfering with my social interactions."
"I can't sleep at night."
"I'm always afraid I will miss out on something if I'm not constantly on my social media."
"I'm checking for new messages all the time. It's an obsession."

Leaders are struggling with digital device etiquette in business meetings. Parents are struggling with smartphones at the dinner table or on the family vacation.

I was recently training a group of executives in the UK, where a female leader told me that she had a 20-year-old intern who was constantly on his phone. She reached out to him, said she noticed he was constantly on his phone and asked him if he felt like he was addicted to it. His reply: "Yes, I am addicted, and I'd like your help. Can you please set some ground rules for me?"

Being born digital does not mean that everything digital is okay and under control. So, the takeaway for leaders, teachers, and parents from this exercise is, that while the majority of our youngsters are fine with their devices and smartphone addiction, quite a large minority are not, and they might need your help.

4.3
PHUBBING — IGNORING PEOPLE

Are we overusing our smartphones? Yes, some people are, and in Chapter 6 we will deep dive into the impact of social media on our mental well-being, especially on youngsters. Here, I'd like to talk about the changing social norms that affect all of us, even those who don't have a smartphone or barely use it. One of the most fundamental changes to the way we interact, due to the smartphone, is the following:

Imagine having a conversation with a few people without using a device – all the participants are physically present. These days, it's normal to have a mobile phone in your hand, in your pocket, on your lap, on the table etc. Then in the middle of the conversation somebody gets a message, they feel the phone buzz in their pocket or see the screen light up. Subconsciously they will swipe the phone, take a look at the message, maybe type a quick response, then put the phone away and join the conversation again. This can happen in just a few seconds, it is very quick, it is subconscious, and most people don't even realize they're doing it; checking out of a conversation and then checking back in again.

There is a relatively new word to describe this behavior; it's called 'phubbing'. The official definition is, "the act of ignoring someone in a social setting and looking at your phone instead of paying attention." Most people do this in one form or another. You might not do it when you're having a romantic dinner but almost everyone does it in a conference room, a business meeting, or among a larger group of friends in a bar. I used to take offence at this behavior if I was delivering a keynote or a workshop, because to me (remember, I'm a middle-aged man in his 40s), it appeared ill-mannered. But having read all the research on the actual brain addiction, I realized people act upon impulse, they simply can't help themselves. Paradoxically, phubbing is an act of connecting with people, just not with those physically present. They are being ignored, while attention is focused on someone elsewhere.

At the moment it's the smartphone but in the future, it might be smartwatches or smart glasses (new versions of the infamous Google Glass) or smart contact lenses that will be the phubbing technology of choice.

Phubbing: the act of ignoring someone in a social setting to look at your phone

The bad news is that people who are being 'phubbed', feel more negative about the interaction and[19] less satisfied with the conversation.[20] In relationships it leads to lower marital satisfaction.[21] Even just having a phone present while having a conversation gives people the feeling of being less connected.[22] The research is myriad. One study's title says it all: "*My life has become a major distraction from my cell phone; partner phubbing and relationship satisfaction among romantic partners.*"[23]

A fun mini-research exercise everyone can do is to look around in any situation where there is social interaction taking place. Look at the amount of phubbing. I'm always struck, not by the activity itself, but the subconscious nature of it.

One of the problems is that other people can't see what the phubbers are doing on their smartphone. Are they looking for directions on Google Maps? Reading a newspaper? Watching a Netflix series? I think phubbing would be less alienating if we could see what phubbers are doing. I don't mean we need to start reading their private messages, but just understanding what it is that makes them choose to be on their device rather than be in the present with those around them. Think of the people in a train not too many years ago. Looking around, you could see what people were doing: reading a book, a newspaper, a work report or trying to study. The transparency of the actions makes the situation less alienating.

My life has become a major distraction from my cell phone

What is the next phase for a world of work full of phubbers? During the first two decades of this century, HR experts were very much about exploring everything digital and in many cases, over-digitizing the world of work. In the 2020s it will be more about a digital balance at work. Two examples:

DEVICE FREE MEETINGS / VACATIONS

Silicon Valley is leading the way with device-free meetings using good old pen and paper. These are proven to be more productive, and people feel more included.[24] I have been to offices which have device racks in meeting rooms so participants can put their devices away – and simultaneously charge them. The Facebook office in London even has a device rack in the restroom and signs on the walls prohibiting the use of laptops in the restroom stalls (this is not a joke, I was there myself!).

There are also employers who encourage their people to be offline during their vacation. Some employers switch off the work email for employees on a beach,[25] others give a bonus

for not using a device and these can vary from hundreds to thousands of dollars.[26] This might feel a bit like parents paying for their teen's driver's license if they don't smoke throughout high school, but I think it's fascinating to see how employers are stepping up.

THE RIGHT TO BE OFFLINE

In the 2010s, governments and unions around the world have implemented policies where employees have the right to be offline or the right to ignore work-related messages during their private time. Several multinationals have followed suit. Companies like T-Mobile and Volkswagen switch off the work email server after hours to protect their employees. Volkswagen's employees in Germany do not receive any messages between 6:15pm and 7am on weekdays and weekends – although senior management is excluded.

STRATEGIC TAKEAWAY

It's time for a no-phubbing culture and although it is far from the case at the moment, leaders have to lead by example. In my experience it is the executives in meetings who do most of the phubbing, thus sending a clear signal to their own people right in front of them: this message is more important than you.

4.4
THE FUTURE: COUNTER TREND, DIGITAL BUTLERS & APATHY

During the infamous pandemic lockdowns many groups of people, from office workers to students, exprienced what it is like to connect virtually – and only virtually – with their colleagues and fellow learners.

Although there were quite a lot of studies on remote working and remote studying before Covid, they were all microscopic in size compared to the data the pandemic lockdowns gave us. The research is conclusive: for the vast majority of people, working / studying remotely resulted in a decrease in productivity, creativity and mental health (much more on the latter in chapter 6).[27]

But what is the right balance here? This topic is driving a lot of reflection and experimentation in practice. For example, I have clients that went fully back to the office after Covid and others that have closed 80% of the office space they operated pre-Covid. Exciting times for HR professionals and people studying the future of (remote) working, but what can we practically expect to happen next?

FULL ANALOG COUNTER TREND

During the 2010s there was a steady trend towards a digital balance through rules, regulation and legislation from organizations and governments, but also new social norms from individuals and groups of people. Simply put, this is a sign that these technologies are maturing and are finding their place in our lives. But to some, this is not enough. There is a small, but growing, countertrend to embrace a full analog, no-devices-anywhere, approach.

In the last decade, the Millennial generation launched social hacks like 'phone stacking' (a stack of phones in a social setting – the first one to touch their phone has to pay a round of drinks) and organized mobile-free parties. Cities around the world are experimenting with so-called smartphone sidewalks and device free sidewalks as a countermeasure against the 'digital zombies' – people who are so engrossed in looking at the screen of their smartphone, they are not paying attention to where they're walking and are bumping into others. Several cities have put stickers on sidewalks encouraging

back at the office, like in the 'good old' analog days. In contrast, Hedge, a video software scale-up, closed all its offices mid-pandemic and announced employees would continue working remotely for the foreseeable future.

Organizations have to be prepared for their clients, stakeholders and partners to be from all areas of the spectrum when it comes to working remotely. Some will be fully virtual and others will still expect a face-to-face meeting, even if that means flying to the other side of the world for a cup of coffee and a Powerpoint presentation. I do expect there'll be significant experimentation and continuing research in order to reach a consensus on best working practices before the end of this decade.

users to 'look up' from their device. Why? Because there have been cases of pedestrians falling down a flight of stairs or into busy intersections. It might sound like madness but google 'cell phone related pedestrian deaths' and you'll see this is a serious issue.

The conversation around 'how can we make this less digital?' is omnipresent and it is not just driven by the older generation or analog industries. No, it is actually young people and tech companies that are leading the debate (see the Time Well Spent movement in Chapter 6). For organizations that have (partly) missed the digital train of the first two decades of the 21st century, this is great news. They can embrace this counter trend and be fully in tune with the times.

We also saw this counter trend during the Covid lockdowns. A striking example was David Solomon, the Goldman Sachs CEO, who said mid-lockdown that post-pandemic, all employees would be required to return to the office, calling working from home "an aberration that we are going to correct as soon as possible."[28] No remote working, not even experimenting with finding a digital balance; simply everyone

DIGITAL BUTLER

Digital technology might help us to find our own personal digital balance. Right now, there are hundreds of apps which will help with digital addiction. These apps track how much you use a device and will (partly) switch devices off, or they will guide you away from social media and offer suggestions for content that help create peace of mind, e.g. Calm or Headspace.

What is your electric knife?

The near future will see the development of the next generation of digital assistants: our digital butler James from Chapter 3. These will help us find our own digital balance, by not disturbing us or making us phub, by filtering content that we really want and need and tuning in to our emotions. Please be aware that in the beginning they will interrupt us and want our attention. They'll make a lot of mistakes and will irritate us as they learn how best to support our needs and requirements. Gradually digital assistants will get smarter, keep their distance and actually protect us from phubbing, reducing the likelihood of addictive behavior. This differs signficantly from a TV that screams for more screentime, or a smartphone and its apps that want to lock its users in as much as possible. Like the very best butlers, the digital assistant will see and hear everything it needs to but act with the utmost discretion!

APATHY

When a technology matures it moves to the background of our perception, it becomes just a part of our lives, and we don't feel the necessity to discuss the existence of it anymore. In the future, a moment will come when all the digital technology we are so excited and worried about today will be like the book printing press. We discuss the content of books, but not the book printing technology itself.

This shift will be accelerated when the hardware itself becomes less relevant. For example, smartphone development will be focused on our personal digital identity in our own digital environment, an identity and environment that will be omnipresent and always with us. Whether we access it via a smartphone, computer, smart watch, car or any other future technology, they will just be tools to access the digital side of ourselves and society. The distinction between the digital and the analog will disappear from the user's perspective. We won't think about the technology itself anymore.

You can draw a historic comparison to the automobile and the radio. When car radios hit the market in the 1920s, people deemed them too dangerous. Both law makers and most of the general public thought radios were a dangerous distraction and claimed they caused accidents – this actually led to a car radio ban in some parts of the US in the 1930s.[29] Both technologies were so new, so exciting, and so all-engrossing, it was thought to be impossible to drive and listen to radio at the same time. As time went by, the technology matured and soon it became impossible to buy a car without a radio as a standard feature.

A final thought. Some of the new technologies will become what I call 'an electric knife'. The electric knife is a relic from the 1960s and 1970s where the futuristic vision of the kitchen led to one too many appliances becoming electric. Our current era of digital transformation will have its own share of electric knives. Just because we can digitalize something, does not mean we should.

STRATEGIC TAKEAWAY

Organizations can develop several future strategies. For the short-term, adapt to the wave of the digital balance counter trend, which will become more prevalent in the coming decade. For the long-term, wait for the development of digital butlers. And a relevant question: which of our new digital products and services have the most potential to become the 'electric knife'? Just because it can be digitalized, doesn't mean it should.

4.5

DIGITAL BALANCE AS A LUXURY

Smartphones and access to the internet became a commodity for all layers of society in the 2010s and most people globally. The unconnected minority will be connected in the 2020s and already in several countries, 'access to the internet' has been implemented as a human right.[30] One consequence is that in countries like the Netherlands and the UK, bailiffs cannot take your computer when you have not paid your debts. Having a device to connect you to the internet is now a basic human need.

It's not so long ago that – and I am old enough to remember – computers were extremely expensive, and the first generation of mobile phones were only for the rich. Being connected 24/7 was a luxury. Now we see the opposite. Rich people are turning away from technology and now not being connected is becoming a luxury. A few examples:

CUSTOMER SERVICE

Most, if not all of my clients struggle with finding a perfect digital balance in their strategies. It is one of the big questions of the first half of the 21st century. Although I don't believe in perfection, I do have an example that comes pretty close, although sadly this service was discontinued, due to its overwhelming popularity and costs.

The service I am referring to is the Mayday button, which was built into Amazon's premium line of Fire and Kindle products from 2014 to 2018. This button could be pressed anytime you needed help with the product. Customers were then instantly connected with a real human Amazon representative via a live video feed, where customers could see the representative but not the other way round. The average response time was a whopping 9.7 seconds. The Mayday feature was hugely popular. Amazon customers were sharing their love on social media, labelling it "the best feature ever." Amazon reported quite a few users 'misused' the Mayday button for non-product related questions. Amazon representatives were asked for restaurant advice, how to get through a difficult Angry Birds level, and to sing 'Happy Birthday' to toddlers. Amazon gave their employees permission to answer these questions as long as they were not offensive.

Mayday was a digital connection from a digital company but with a real human being and its popularity showed there's a need for a digital balance feature like this. Organizations should ask themselves: what is the Mayday feature for our product or service?

TOURISM & EDUCATION

One of the first industries to start actively looking for a digital balance was the tourist industry in the early 2010s. As the masses started bringing their smartphones to the beach to check cat videos on Facebook and write work emails, most tourist destinations responded with free-fast-WiFi everywhere. But soon, the counter trend started, and luxury resorts were the first to implement device-free policies, a bit like the dress codes some have in their restaurants. The 5-star Chiva-Som resort in Thailand only allows devices in guest rooms, not anywhere else. The luxury spa resort hotel Villa Stéphanie in Germany has a kill switch in every hotel room that activates a copper grid within the walls to divert any incoming connections. The hotel manager, who compares our addiction to our digital devices to smoking, has reported that half the guests use the switch during their stay.[31]

That's not surprising. Because if you check your emails and social media messages every day of the family holiday, are you really on vacation? Physically yes, but mentally as well? A friend of mine decided last year to stay at home for the summer holidays but switch off all his devices for two weeks. He came to the conclusion that he had more of a vacation, was more rested than he had ever been in all those years of traveling the world with his devices.

Of course, there are technical solutions out there. My favorite is a brilliant travel app called White Spots, which shows on a map where the nearest 'white spot' is – a place where there is no cell phone coverage. What a brilliant idea, to use your device to get to a place where it won't receive a signal!

The tourism industry is surprisingly similar to the world of education. Schools have struggled for years to ensure their ICT equipment and education is up to par. Governments, NGOs and individuals have stepped in to help schools equip themselves for the 21st century: let's have screens instead of a chalk board! And as smart school boards, school tablets, learning apps, and IT education are maturing in our schools, the counter trend has started. There are private schools without any digital devices, no WiFi, even no IT education, with the school buildings located in natural surroundings. This might sound like a basic, cheap, old school analog version of education, but it is not. On the contrary, the schools are very expensive. Schools like *The Brightworks School* and the *Waldorf School of the Peninsula* in the US cost over $25,000 per year, schools that are most popular with parents who work in… yes, Silicon Valley.[32] The private *Acorn School* in London (£11,000 a year) has policies that go beyond its American counterparts; surfing the web both at home *and* school is not allowed until the age of 16. Students and parents must commit to that.

Misconception: people only want smooth sailing and speedy efficiency

RESTAURANTS

In the restaurant business we see a different kind of digital balance. In fast food chains there is no digital balance. They are rapidly replacing human beings with devices: order via a screen, pay with a card only, look on a screen to see when your order is ready, pick up your order from a counter. There's hardly any human interaction. Yes, there are still people in the kitchen,

It's a common misconception that human beings only want smooth sailing and speedy efficiency

but what if these could be automated as well? Would it matter to the customers?

One would think that 'slow' food restaurants would adopt a bit of this automation as well. For example, the process of ordering via a digital device. Wouldn't it be easier and more efficient for everyone involved to do this via a screen? The answer is yes, but customers don't appear to want this. Not everything in life is about efficiency. The ambience, the conversation with your server, the ordering if you're with a large group, the menu recommendations, it's all part of the restaurant experience. It's a common misconception that human beings only want smooth sailing and speedy efficiency.

I do think some restaurants in the 2020s will offer both options. Customers will get the choice to order via screen, or if you feel like receiving a personal recommendation press a button – like the one above your head in an airplane – and the server will happily come to you. Digital balance a la carte! During the pandemic we saw some restaurants begin to adopt a digital rather than physical menu approach, though customers were still actually served in person.

POSTAL DELIVERY

The growth of online shopping in the 2010s had already been spectacular and then Covid hit the world. This was a KABOOM! for e-commerce: in most markets the share of e-commerce of total sales doubled in size.[33] Although the pandemic did increase the quantity side of online shopping, on the quality side, not much happened. Yes, there were a few luxury retail stores that connected online buyers with physical instore employees, but those initiatives were already in place pre-Covid.

With all the current technology, a fully automated experience in the future is a viable possibility. Here's a scenario:

In a few years' time, your restroom will have a sensor that senses you are almost out of toilet paper and so it will automatically order toilet paper for you. Of course, it will be one of your favorite brands, for a great price. This toilet paper will then be automatically loaded by a robot into a self-driving electric car that will drive to your house. Another delivery robot will put it on your doorstep. Maybe you will then have a household robot which will put it in your restroom.

Now this might sound quite sci-fi, but we will already see parts of this scenario play out in the next decade and I think it's brilliant. I have yet to meet anyone who enjoys buying toilet paper (please do let me know if you do!). The above scenario would be a luxury hotel-like fea-ture – never run out of toilet paper again or have to purchase those bulky packages. Wonderful!

But only because it's toilet paper

I don't want a feature like this for my suits. I don't want a sensor and algorithm deciding I need a new suit. That I open my closet on a Tuesday morning and there is a new suit hanging there. I like buying my suits myself, going into town with my wife, feeling the fabric, having a conversation with an expert, drinking a cup of coffee, enjoying the experience. I don't want that to be automated.

STRATEGIC TAKEAWAY

The question business owners must ask themselves is, what is my toilet paper and what is my business suit? Then automate the toilet paper a bit more but humanize the suit more as well. Hire people with superb soft skills for the latter and charge extra, as this is the new luxury.

A shared experience is much more valuable than something experienced just by yourself

4.6
PRACTICING PATIENCE IN A WORLD THAT'S SPEEDING UP

During the past 10 years I have heard the following cliché a gazillion times: "The world is changing much faster than it used to!" One of the main arguments for this statement is that the pace of technological adaptation is speeding up. Meaning, the time for a new technology to reach a mass market is becoming shorter and shorter. For example, it took the television 20 years to reach a mass audience, the internet 15 years, and the tablet only 5 years.[34]

Adaptation is not adoption

And yes, this cliché is true. Many innovative businesses might be excited about this, but society is not, because society needs time to adapt to change. Technologies take decades to land in society. Take the television and the huge impact it had on households in the 1950s and 1960s. It changed the physical design of living rooms, it changed family leisure time and it led to significant questions. Would you leave the television on if friends and family came over? Could you have dinner and watch television at the same time? What's the best distance to sit away from the television? How much television is healthy to watch? What's the role of the television in education, or in business? It took the experts decades to do the research, observe, discuss and start to formulate answers. I grew up in the 1980s and there was still a medical discussion going on about whether it was safe to watch television in total darkness or would it be better for your eyes if a small light was left on in the corner of the room.

So, while the smartphone has taken the world by storm, this does not mean society has adapted to it. People using a product is not the same as societal embrace of that product. To put it philosophically, *adaptation is not adoption*. It will be another twenty years before it has fully landed and that is only if we stop adding major features now.

Although most smart people know this, my clients want answers NOW on new technology "otherwise we'll be the next Kodak!" Parents also want immediate answers: "My kids are struggling with all this technology right now, what does the research say I should do?" The realistic answer is that we just don't know yet. We must give it time. It will probably be another ten to twenty years before we fundamentally know the good and the bad and we have to accept that the decades ahead of us will be filled with trial and error, discussions and uncertainty.

STRATEGIC TAKEAWAY

Leaders have to be resilient in the face of the 'innovate or die' rhetoric from the disruption gurus. Zooming out, society still adapts slowly to technological innovation, so yes, there is time.

4.7

THE FUTURE OF HUMAN WORK

The elephant in the room when it comes to finding a digital balance is the question: won't we all be replaced by machines? It is one of the biggest, most interesting questions of our time. Luckily, it's also a question that is centuries old, as the fear of being replaced by new technology is as old as technology itself. Remember the book printing press worries dating back 500 years ago, that it would put the monks who copied books by hand out of a job and they would lose their purpose?

Then there is the "But wait, this time it's different!" argument that we hear from many experts in the media. They argue that the technology being developed today cannot be compared to technological innovation in the past. The interesting thing is, that "this time it's different" is also a very old argument that's been used for over a hundred years. So how about zooming out and asking ourselves: is it truly different for us, or does every generation define the future technology they're facing as uniquely different, disruptive, and not comparable to anything that has happened before?

Since the beginning of the 20th century, every generation has its own fear of technology taking jobs. In 1930, the economist J.M. Keynes[35] predicted a 15-hour work week around the year 2000, due to technology taking over our jobs. In the 1960s, a US Senate committee report predicted a 14-hour work week by the year 2000. Indeed, even one hour less than Keynes.[35] After a quiet 1970s, the fear of future technology and unemployment started snowballing again in the 1980s, with the PC, the internet and the rise of algorithms and AI. Politicians, scientists, journalists seemed to be tumbling over each other to provide worst-case scenario predictions. In 2013, researchers from the University of Oxford published a paper predicting huge job losses due to automation: by 2030, 48% of our current jobs were at risk of being replaced by technology – the majority of those even at 'high risk'.[36] This research led the BBC to develop an online job loss calculator based on the Oxford research: just type in your job and you could discover the likelihood of it being replaced by technology. If you are an accountant, the tool will tell you that your job has a risk of 95% of being automated. An HR manager on the other hand has only a 32% chance of being automated.[37]

So, am I going to predict a 14 or a 15-hour work week? No. If there is one lesson to be learned from history, it is that humans excel in keeping themselves busy and are endlessly creative in developing new jobs and even whole industries. This is not to say that we won't see local and regional temporary unemployment in certain sectors due to the advances of technology. But these will be comparable to the

The more digital society
gets, the more we want real
human contact

temporary unemployment caused by coal mines or weaving factories closing.

It is possible, though, that we'll see a push for the four-day work week. There are quite a few experiments with positive outcomes, primarily in Europe and mostly for other reasons than to compensate for job losses due to automation. Spain launched a nationwide trial in 2021: a three-year, €50 million project, with hundreds of organizations participating.[38] Maybe we'll get to see the four-day work week being institutionalized a hundred years after the five-day work week was (1932).

A surgeon might be automated, the nurse is not

Most experts agree the automation we can predict is like factory workers being replaced by machines: it is the automation of repetitive, boring tasks.[39] And that leads to an interesting follow-up question: how many truly fun, engaging, immersive, creative tasks have been replaced by technology? How many dream jobs have disappeared throughout history? Yes, there are still communities which mourn the loss of jobs due to the closure of the mines, decades ago. But is it really the task itself which is mourned? No, it was being employed, making an honest living, being part of a working community, being part of society, being part of a greater good, having colleagues. In short: having a purpose.

If we shift the focus to new kinds of future jobs instead of resisting technological progress and delaying an inevitable process, it becomes a different discussion. What will the jobs of the future be? The obvious answer is, of course, jobs related to all this new technology. For example,

in the US in 2018, more than 350,000 people were working in the solar energy industry.[40] Fun examples of future jobs that are likely to come in one form or another: 6G antenna engineer, postal drone flight programmer, vertical garden farmer and VR avatar designer. It's a great exercise to try to find a few of your own. If you find it difficult, involve a few teenagers in your brainstorming. In my experience, they have the best ideas.

But what if we look beyond these 'obvious' new technology jobs? This is where it gets interesting. I believe we'll see three categories of new jobs:

ONE – HIGH-TOUCH PEOPLE JOBS.

For people with great soft skills. The more technological and digital society gets, the more we want real human contact. Harvard did an elaborate study in the mid-2010s, and they could already see this in the numbers.[41] As technology is out-pacing us in speed and efficiency, people skills become the great differentiator. And this is another example of the 'toilet paper or suit' choice, that organizations have to make.

The fitness industry is a great example. There seem to be two roads to take, the first being the all-automated low-budget chains, with automatic check-ins, virtual instructors and group classes taught via screens. On the other side are the high-touch fitness clubs with the best personal trainers with great soft skills and a well-developed EQ, where clients get a personalized program and treatment.

And this real people contact is a fundamental, unchangeable human need. Think of an office building. It's quite easy to have a digital reception desk where human beings have been replaced by screens. Visitors can check-in, get a parking ticket and a coffee. But who wants to walk into a reception area without real human contact? Which company would like its customers to be welcomed by a screen?

TWO – JOBS ASSOCIATED WITH CARING FOR OUR MENTAL WELL-BEING.

Chapter 6 is dedicated to the trend that taking care of our mental well-being will become as normal as eating healthily and doing sports. The jobs here will be done mostly by people – with some help from an app or digital assistant. It will be actual people who will really take care of us, in the same way our children are being taught by a human teacher and not by a virtual professor. Currently the jobs associated with our mental well-being are psychologists, psychiatrists, therapists, coaches, yoga and meditation teachers. I fundamentally believe we will see many more categories of professionals who will make sure that we are happy, resilient, and mentally balanced. In the 20th century, we have learned to take care of our physical well-being by exercising and eating healthily. The 21st century will be where we take care of our own mental health, our networks and society's mental well-being – for all ages and every layer of society. Think of the mental equivalent of a fitness club, PE class in school or a standing desk with an ergonomic chair in a modern office. Much more on this in Chapter 6.

THREE – THE UNKNOWN JOBS.

This is actually quite a strange category, because these are the non-tech jobs of the future about which we know nothing as yet – the so-called 'unknown unknowns'. Unfortunately, these jobs cannot be predicted, but there are wonderful historic examples of this.

My favorite is the profession of nail technician. Before the 1970s, this job did not exist, only the rich and famous had a 'manicurist'. But then, during the 1970s in the US, Vietnamese refugees started nail salons.[42] It soon became a huge success and in 1980, the US Bureau of Labor Statistics recognized it as a profession.[43] The manicure and nail salon trend spread globally. Now, 50 years later, it is a multi-billion-dollar industry which employs millions of people. As an example, in the US alone, more than 400,000 people earn a living as a nail technician,[44] while the whole US coal mining industry employs less than 70,000 people.[45]

So, looking into the future, I'd love the whole societal and political discussion about the future of work to be turned into a simple question: how are we going to keep ourselves busy? I truly believe that we can, and we will. But are we going to fight automation and be reactive and wait for jobs to be lost? Or will we be proactive with a positive approach? The result will probably be along the same lines, though the latter approach will speed things up and create less uncertainty among the public.

STRATEGIC TAKEAWAY

Invest in people, services, and industries which are high-touch soft skill industries. A surgeon might be automated, the nurse is not. Keep an eye out for jobs associated with our mental well-being. Leaders should not be afraid there will be a lack of jobs for people in the future, because we will create new ones. So how about creating a new category of jobs yourself?

5.
FUTURE ETHICS

5.1 Who's responsible for this?
5.2 Jumping into the ethics vacuum
5.3 Ethics in the workplace
5.4 Moral licensing, purpose washing, and cancel culture
5.5 Puritanism fallacy
5.6 Indirect activism & nudge the nudgers

INTRODUCTION

Throughout the previous chapters, there were many references forward to this chapter as many topics addressed beg for an ethical angle. I actually wanted to make this Chapter 1, as its subject is the most fundamental of all: ethics. Especially as ethics is intrinsically linked to the climate crisis – the biggest, most fundamental global challenge of this century.

But this is not Chapter 1, this is Chapter 5. And the reason for that is what I call 'the vegetarian problem'.

Imagine a group of friends who all eat meat. Then one day, a group member decides to become a vegetarian. Let's call him Jeff. At the next social get together, Jeff shares with the group he has become a vegetarian, because he wants to reduce his carbon footprint as he is very worried about global warming. What do you think the first psychological response from his friends is? Will they:

a.   Like him more, because he is doing something noble for the planet.
b.   Like him the same, because eating meat is not relevant to their friendship.
c.   Like him less, because he makes the meat eaters feel bad about themselves.

You have probably guessed correctly, most people's first response is answer c. Instead of feeling proud of Jeff and praising him, their primary emotional response is along the lines of: "Do you think I don't care about the planet?!" And: "Are you implying I am a bad person because I do eat meat?"

The 'vegetarian problem' is this emotional negative first response to an ethical deed. It can also be observed when people raise an ethical topic in a business meeting. Also here the first response is often a negative and defensive one. It is not that people rationally disagree with the 'vegetarian', it is emotions that are the drivers of this response.

So what can the Jeffs of this world do? Research has shown that the best way to talk to a group of meat eaters about not eating animals is to approach the topic indirectly and from a non-moral angle, for example: "it's great for your health!"

Once the discussion is underway, then slowly the moral / ethical justifications of vegetarianism can be addressed, preferably by the meat eaters. Activists might dislike this indirect approach, but if the outcome is what matters most, it is strongly suggested to give it a go.

And by making 'Future Ethics' Chapter 5 instead of Chapter 1, I hope I have done just that and you, dear reader, will stay with me. As you have made it here through the first four chapters, we can now deep dive into the future of ethics, which I define as: "the art of doing the right thing."

Ethics: The art of doing the right thing

With all the challenges the world is facing, 'ethics' is arguably the most important topic of all. In fact, just global warming alone has the potential to become a global crisis of unprecedented proportions that will deem all other topics in this book trivial. Add to that challenges like increasing social inequality, an ongoing decline in global freedom, extreme political polarisation, diversity & inclusion challenges and one can be become quite fatalistic. As an optimist, I think it's never too late and we can still save ourselves. Hopefully this book will speed up all the future discussions you will have on ethics – good luck!

5.1

WHO'S RESPONSIBLE FOR THIS?

We now live in a time where people are more focused than ever on finding and pursuing their purpose in life, while aligning their needs and desires with what's 'right'. For most of our ancestors, ethics were not a concern for the average person — let alone being consistently and publicly debated. For them, a guiding set of ethical rules was provided or imposed by a dominant religion, a monarchy, an aristocracy, or a ruler like an emperor, dictator, or enlightened despot. Think of Christianity's Ten Commandments or Aristotle's justification of a monarchy — where a king has practical wisdom and virtue superior to that of his subjects.

The 20th century saw the individualization of ethics. The influence of the established religions on society declined, monarchies served mostly as fodder for the tabloids and the world had fewer dictators than ever before. With the individualization of society, ethics became more and more the responsibility of each of us. In effect, ethics from a bottom-up perspective. In theory, this should be positive, but in practice it is incredibly challenging, as the views and opinions of individual people with regard to ethical issues can vary wildly. For this reason we often see ethics and the discussion of key ethical themes sidelined when debating legislation, regulation, standards, codes, and policies. These debates determine the boundaries of what society can operate in, and because these laws and rules are both complex and omnipresent, it's less challenging to use them as the guiding principles when making ethical decisions. Many business leaders have 'outsourced' thinking about ethics to their legal department: "Just give us the legislation and the rules and we'll be fine." This follows the precepts of the Friedman Doctrine, a theory coined in 1970 by the famous economist Milton Friedman. He argued that 'the business of business is business', and that organizations have no responsibility to society in general.

Once a social norm has been taken away, it will rarely and only slowly return

Which would be fine if following the laws and the rules always works. But unfortunately, that's not always the case.

Many laws and rules have an opposite effect to what they were put in place for. Dan Ariely, Professor of Psychology and Behavioral Economics, describes a classic example of what goes wrong in practice. A daycare center in Israel had a problem with parents picking up their children late, after the official closing time. This forced their personnel to work overtime.

To make parents be on time they imposed a new rule where they would be fined if they picked up their kids late. A perfectly logical solution according to the management, but did this lead to better behavior in the parents? No, the number of parents who picked up their children late doubled.

What's at play here? Before the fine was introduced, the daycare and the parents had a social contract with social norms – the 'punish-ment' for coming late was an emotional feeling of guilt. Then the social norms were replaced by market norms and guilt was replaced by a monetary exchange.

The business of business is business

The daycare realized they had made a mistake and after a few weeks removed the fee. Did things return to the way they were before? No, the number of latecomers stayed where it was (double the initial number). Why? Once a social norm has been taken away, it will rarely and only slowly return.

The economist, lecturer and government adviser Tomáš Sedláček explains in his book, *The Economics of Good and Evil*, that society is focusing so much on laws and rules, people have forgotten why the rules were implemented in the first place. For example, from an ethical perspective everyone agrees with taxes as they pay for our schools, hospitals, roads, and other social necessities. This is what Sedláček calls the 'goal'. To ensure taxes are paid, there are a series of 'means' in place like tax legislation and trade agreements. Yet over time more focus has been placed on the 'means' and people seem to have forgotten that the taxes were originated with an ethical goal.

This century, the list of multinationals that pay none or hardly any tax on their profits has become extensive. When these companies are asked about this, they always reply that they don't do anything illegal and that they are obeying all necessary international laws and treaties: "it's not tax evasion, but tax optimisation." In short, they are playing by the rules. Sedláček says this is only half of the discussion, because again we are only focused on the means and not the goals as well.

And society wants to talk about the goals – ethics – as well. The societal turmoil of the late 2010s and early 2020s, with protests about global warming, inequality and corrupt governments, clearly shows that we are at a turning point of an ethics shift. The arguments 'we are just playing by the rules' and 'we are operating in the framework that we are given' are not enough anymore. Underneath the unrest is the need for answers to fundamental questions. What kind of world do we want to live in? What are the ethical goals we base our decisions on?

The Covid pandemic might have pressed pause on practically discussing challenges like global warming and (social) inequality, but these challenges have returned like a boomerang, squarely hitting many unprepared organizations and leaders. The downside of the pandemic was that many discussions were halted as we had to "fix Covid first!" The upside is that it showed us we can adapt to and tackle a global crisis. That is to say, when the smartest people in the world – with almost unlimited monetary resources – join forces and work towards a common goal. No one predicted we'd have multiple working vaccines within a year of the first outbreak. When Covid was first acknowledged, experts were predicting four to seven years for the first vaccines to be developed.

This raises another question: how bad does global warming have to get until we see a similar response? Or how big should inequality become before we witness any substantial national and international social reform?

STRATEGIC TAKEAWAY

Leaders have to look beyond rules & regulation and understand *why* these are put in place. A future proof leader must be able to talk about rules & regulation and be able to address this in their organizational strategy. A great start is to ask why one's own organization exists. Is it just to make money – or is there an underlying goal?

5.2

JUMPING INTO THE ETHICS VACUUM

With ethics buried within a society that's driven by laws and regulation it's inevitable that there will be an ethics vacuum. If ethics are vital in helping solve the challenges the world is facing, the question arises, who is responsible for ensuring ethics remain key in society? Who will 'fill' the ethics vacuum? There are potentially three key scenarios that could play out simultaneously in the near future.

Who will be the Greta Thunberg of the business world in the coming decade?

The first is a focus on the traditional, strong, male leader who tells us in bold and plain language what is wrong or right. And – always – HE is the answer, the solution, and the savior. Globally we see these archetypal older gentlemen that use hackneyed black and white, us vs. them rhetoric, jump into the ethics vacuum. Although most of them act like they came straight out of *Dr. Strangelove* (a classic political satire movie), real people cast real votes for them. The reason is that voters believe a strong leader will take care of them and protect them: "He will take care of our country, my community, my family and me." In a complicated, ambiguous world, where reality is blurred and the truth is gray instead of black and white, it's a relief if a leader can make sense of it all with some simple rhetoric.

The problem, of course, is that we often discover this style of leader tends not to care too much about ethics, or ethically-driven causes such as taking care of the planet. They mostly care about their own circle and pursue a short-term, political survivalist strategy. In the end, this kind of leadership is not sustainable – as we'll either destroy the planet or end up in a

World War III scenario. But what's the alternative? As the demand for belonging and being taken care of will only grow in the coming years, there is a fair chance we will see an equally strong leadership style emerge but an empathetic one – a strong woman or man who is more inclusive, and cares for the planet. Though inclusivity wouldn't hurt the short-term goals organizations have, as many of those old-fashioned saviors would argue. We know from organizational psychology research that a more empathetic and inclusive culture leads to higher employee satisfaction. And satisfied employees work harder and are ill less often, which will please even the most profit-driven leader.

A second scenario sees more and more people finding an ethical framework within new forms of spirituality. In the secularizing West, people might not be traditionally religious, but they are increasingly attracted to the other forms of spirituality like yoga and meditation. Interestingly, in a US study among people who practice yoga, researchers found that almost two-thirds of people who practice yoga changed their primary reason for practicing: they came in for the physical well-being, but stayed because of the spirituality. Many academics agree that yoga – and meditation – fit the criteria of a religion. The ethical framework of new spirituality like yoga is different from traditional religions. The Western interpretation of these ancient practices is very much an individualistic one, focused on the self, and less on the collective.

Despite not fitting the traditional criteria of a spiritual movement, the rise of modern conspiracy thinking, whether it's the anti-vax movement or the QAnon conspiracy (with the mysterious Q as a sort of new messiah), can also be defined as a (quasi) religion. Conspiracy theory thinking always provides a clear distinction between right and wrong, good and evil, and has simple, black and white answers to many complicated matters. Just like a religion, it gives the believer a framework to hold onto.

This makes sense, as if the rational, scientific, and technocratic world does not provide many people with definite answers and a spelled out ethical framework, then maybe the spiritual, esoteric, and conspiritual can. This shift is not a truly global one. Although Western countries and China are simultaneously secularizing more, the rest of the world is becoming more religious. Currently 84% of the global population identifies with a religious group and experts expect this number to increase to 87% by 2050.

The third scenario envisages the world of business proactively adopting ethics. Not simply because they are intrinsically motivated to do so, but because increasingly people ask it from them: customers, employees, future talent, investors et al. In a representative global study, 80% of respondents agreed to the statement that organizations have to lead when solving world problems. That is right: *lead*. Not playing a part, not following the rules, no: LEAD. And that is quite an eye-opener for many organizations after decades of following the rules Milton Friedman-style.

The wave of global street protests from the climate protest, to Black Lives Matter, from school strikes to the Yellow Vest events – can be seen as a societal outcry: "please take care of us!" and "please take care of the planet." This message is not only targeted at politicians, but also at the world of business. The question is if the world of for-profit business can step up to the plate and practically lead when it comes to ethics.

An increasing number of experts agree that the early 21st century marks the end of classic capitalism (neoliberalism) and that we will switch to a new socio-economic model. In 2020, even the Financial Times (known for defending neoliberalism), surprised many with an editorial in which the newspaper marked the end of neoliberalism and predicted a social economy that is more regulated.

I do believe we will see a fundamental transition soon and that ethical leaders will play a key role. The media and the general public can't wait for a leader like that. Elon Musk was hailed in the early days of Tesla as the embodiment of a synthesis of Greenpeace and Microsoft. But this was tarnished somewhat when Musk began focussing on the billionaire space race and flirted with the most polluting cryptocurrency of all: Bitcoin. This is a fun one to discuss over lunch: who will be the Greta Thunberg of the business world in the coming decade?

STRATEGIC TAKEAWAY

One of the characteristics of the turbulent times we live in is caused by our current 'ethics vacuum'. People are actively looking to fill this vacuum by turning to individual spirituality or voting for old-fashioned strong leaders. As these are not sustainable solutions, different kinds of leaders are needed – both in politics and in business. Leaders who actually *lead* when it comes to ethical issues and the problems the world is facing.

5.3
ETHICS IN THE WORKPLACE

Most organizations would like to do more, but struggle with incorporating ethics in their mission/vision statement, in their culture and in their decision making. The reason cited by professionals is most often that day-to-day organizational performance is getting in the way. But there is an underlying problem: we do not know how to have a conversation about ethics. It's not something we've learnt. Nor how to make a sound decision if we speak a different language.

Everybody has a moral compass, unless you have an empathy deficit disorder. Even those we don't think have one do – it's just a compass that is not aligned with ours. In a utopian society or organization all the moral compasses would be aligned and ethical decision making would be a piece of cake. But this is not how it works in the real world. For example, ask a group of professionals to define 'diversity in the workplace' and chances are high that you'll get as many different answers as there are people in the room.

If a decision has to be made, the arguments often become quite emotional and people start to express their arguments in the form of "I strongly feel…", "I wholeheartedly believe…" and "I really think the right thing to do is…"

The discussion becomes an exchange of emotions and, as we have discussed before, feelings are often stronger than facts, which further complicates any discussion on ethics in business. Almost everyone has an opinion on ethics as it primarily concerns issues we care most deeply about. It is not a topic like *supply chain logistics*, where people can easily say: I don't know anything about that, so I don't have an opinion on the subject. In practice within businesses, many ethical conversations stall and are tossed back to the legal department, because 'we have to play by the rules' is the one thing everyone can agree on.

If only we had the knowledge and the skills to talk about ethics and integrate it into our decision making. But we don't. If we look at the education our future leaders are receiving at colleges and universities around the world, ethics is not an integral part of the course. Harvard, for example, describes its business 'Management Degree Program' as follows:

Gain a solid grounding in management theory and practice through foundational subjects, including economics, accounting, finance, strategy, marketing, organizational behavior, and management.

'We have to play by the rules'
is the one thing everyone
can agree on

It has three terms to describe the financial side of management: economics, accounting, finance. But ethics is not a 'foundational' subject. It is not that ethics skills are not being taught to leaders at all, but mostly as an add-on, an optional course, a topic for a guest speaker, an afternoon module in a leadership program or a completely separate degree – at the faculty of philosophy, that is.

With the problems the world is facing in the coming years and decades, this is not enough. So what can organizations do?

We have questionable clients already, so why decline this one?

1. GET OUTSIDE HELP

A great example of this is when I worked with the board of a large European Energy Company. This company has sustainability firmly rooted in its mission, vision and values – and they had so even before Al Gore rang his *Inconvenient Truth* bell. When I discussed ethics with them they shared an ethical challenge they faced and how they had solved it.

It started with their sales team asking the board if it was okay to take a specific business client on. Normally these questions do not reach the board – but this client was a large multinational oil trading company with a questionable reputation when it came to sustainability. On the Wikipedia page of the company the list of 'controversies' was as long as the standard information about their business. In the (recent) past, they had to settle a number of lawsuits and pay fines, but it was perfectly legal to do business with them. The question from the sales team to the board: do we take them on as a client?

The board was split 50/50 on the answer. Half the board members said 'no' as it was a client as far removed from their values as it was possible to be. The other half said 'yes' as they argued a few of their other business clients had questionable reputations as well. It was great business, it was legal and they should be given a fair chance.

So what to do? They sought outside help. A professional expert in ethical decision making sat down with the board and deconstructed arguments from all sides, pointing out a few fallacies. One of them being: "we have accepted a few questionable clients already, so why turn down this one?" If you throw three empty beer cans on the grass next to the trash can, it does not mean you should do that with the fourth as well.

The professional asked them to outline the company's values, mission, and vision and together they determined whether the deconstructed arguments aligned with those. After doing this, the answer became clear and they unanimously agreed to not take on the client.

Then one of the board members suggested creating a press release to try and secure some good PR from the decision. The ethics professional suggested discussing that as well and after a similar process, they decided *not* to have corporate communications put it out there. It wasn't a secret, but it was decided it shouldn't be used as a marketing opportunity.

Securing an external facilitator who is trained in discussing ethics is a great first step for leadership teams. But what about everyday decision making?

2. TRAIN YOURSELF AND YOUR PEOPLE

Even if all business schools around the world made business ethics as important as finance or people management, it would still take decades before their students became the majority of leaders. This leaves organizations only one option: train their people. And if it is not organized for you: train yourself.

Almost all larger organizations have learning and development programs in place for their employees. These programs rarely train ethics skills and if they do, it's a little something extra, the cherry on top of the cake. Or this training is only included because of an externality – like putting privacy on the agenda because of GDPR legislation. The message this conveys is that ethics is (a lot) less important than developing skills in strategy, finance, project management, communication et al.

The question from the sales team to the board: do we take them on as a client?

Organizations which would like to incorporate ethics in all their decision making need a paradigm shift where ethics language and skills become the cake and not just the cherry. To treat ethics the same way as strategy, finance, or project management, allocating ample resources (budget and time). There is a bit of light at the end of the tunnel. I have been contributing to a number of leadership programs where finding the company's purpose and establishing one's own moral compass and business integrity were learning modules.

One of the factors holding companies back in addressing ethics language and skills is that it sounds too vague, too philosophical, or too moralistic. The good news is that it doesn't have to be, and that first steps can be made quite easily.

In a fascinating study by the North Carolina State University, researchers studied how to get IT developers to make more responsible decisions. The study shows that having a 'code of ethics' is less effective than informing developers about critical historical ethical events in the past – such as Volkswagen's dieselgate scandal. The researchers conclude that teaching software developers about ethical situations from the past, and helping them draw parallels between their work and those incidents, is an effective tool to inspire more ethical decision making in a work situation. The principle at work here is that it's easier to practice discussing ethics on a topic not directly related to one's personal life. Remember, these historical examples were real life events, yet the code of ethics is still often conceived as vague.

3. INSTALL A CHIEF ETHICS OFFICER

For larger organizations a logical step is to employ one or more ethics professionals who will make sure ethics are embedded throughout the organization and become part of the decision making culture.

The current challenge is that in most organizations 'ethics' are scattered throughout the company. For example, HR might have a 'diversity officer', the engineering department may have a 'sustainability program manager', legal may have a 'compliance and ethics team' and the IT team may have a 'privacy specialist' onboard. All these experts should be brought together under one umbrella to align and strengthen their impact. It will make it much easier for employees to understand that all these scattered ethical initiatives are part of the same principle: ethics.

Compare it to IT in the 1990s. The IT department was a separate department. Not only in the organizational chart, but also physically. The IT experts were often tucked away in a remote part of the building which the average worker only visited – reluctantly – when their laptop or email stopped working. Organizations gradually realised that IT is an integral part of a company and slowly but steadily, IT made its way up the organizational charts – and physically from the basement to the C-suite. Nowadays, virtually every larger organization has a CIO (or CDO, or CTO). Let's take a look at the definition:

"A chief information officer, or CIO, is the company executive responsible for the management, implementation, and usability of information and computer technologies. The CIO analyzes how these technologies benefit the company or improve an existing business process, and then integrates a system to realize that benefit or improvement."

Companies need a Chief Ethics Officer

Let's replace 'computer technologies' with 'ethics' in that definition and it is crystal clear that companies need a Chief Ethics Officer. I propose 'CETO' as a brand new acronym: "A chief ethics officer, or CETO, is the company executive responsible for the management, implementation, and usability of ethics in decision making. The CETO analyzes how ethical decision making benefits the company or improves an existing business process, and then integrates ethics to realize that benefit or improvement."

More recently I have encountered 'chief privacy officers' and 'chief sustainability officers'. This is a great start, but these professionals cover only part of the ethical field. I expect the first CETOs to be installed in the 2020s. In discussing this topic with professionals I have met nothing but enthusiasm for the concept of a CETO. Younger employees especially expressed the

'urgent' need for a CETO in their organization. A number even expressed the desire to become one!

The one place I have run into opposition to the CETO concept is in the boardroom. Reactions include: "don't you think I can do that myself?" and "I have a moral compass, I make ethical decisions." Board members see the suggestion of a CETO as a personal attack on their moral compass. I like to compare it to the role of a CFO. Having a finance officer in the board does not mean that the other board members have a lack of financial knowledge. Or that they can outsource any financial challenge to the CFO. No, finance is still part of every board member's skill set and responsibility. The CFO is the specialist in the group, with the ultimate responsibility for this area. Again, replace 'finance' with 'ethics' and it should ease the adaptation of the idea of an ethics professional in the boardroom.

STRATEGIC TAKEAWAY

Leaders should proactively train themselves and their people on ethical language, skills and decision making. Failing to do so will mean a diminished attraction of talent, and the loss of customers and investments. And just as the CIO in the boardroom is a given today, a CETO (Chief Ethical Officer) will be tomorrow, so consider installing one.

EXERCISE

ETHICS EXERCISES

Starting 'a conversation on ethics' with a group of people is a great way to kill the mood, drain the energy from a room, and risk a defensive response. A sensitive topic like this is best approached in an indirect manner, like a game or an exercise. Here are two examples:

1. This game is based on the Golden Balls game show that ran on the BBC in the late 2000s. In the (in)famous final round of the game, two contestants have to battle for a jackpot. They both get two golden balls, one marked 'split' the other one 'steal'. They then have to secretly choose the ball that shows their intentions – the choices are then both revealed.

→ If they both turn out to have chosen 'split' they each get half of the jackpot.
→ If they both chose 'steal' they get nothing.
→ If one chose 'steal' and the other one 'split' the one who chose 'steal' gets everything.

Before the contestants make their decision they get a minute to talk to each other and talk about what they are going to do. For this exercise, the moderator is temporarily the quiz show host and explains the rules. They then split the group into pairs. Give the pairs a nice jackpot –

say $100,000– and one minute to discuss. After the minute they have to decide to split or steal. But no actual golden balls are needed, just have everyone close their eyes and scream out what they will do on the count of three: so, one, two, three… scream answer!

In almost all cases the majority of the group will scream 'split' with only a few 'steals'. The steal people are a good focus for the start of the group discussion. Why did they decide to steal? Most will say they were afraid the other would steal. Or, they would rather leave both with nothing than have the other one win. The moderator can then ask about the conversations the pairs had in which they talked about their intentions.

The underlying theme here is trust. What did they say to be trusted? And what made them trust the other person?
On a rare occasion, everyone will scream 'split'. In this case the modera-

tor can ask which people were seriously thinking about stealing, but in the end did not do it, and why? Another question for a group full of splitters is if they think their choices represent society: do we live in a split or steal society?

The 'golden balls' can then be used as a bridge to have an in-depth conversation on the response from the organizations and leaders to current (or future) ethical dilemmas. Do they have a 'split' or 'steal' response?

What would that mean?

2. *Glad that's not our problem!* It is a lot easier to talk about other organizations and other industries with other ethical issues than one's own. Therefore, one of the most impactful ethics exercises to do is to discuss an ethical issue from another industry or one related to a future technology. One of my favorite topics to discuss in a workshop is the technology called Emotion AI. This is technology that can measure a person's real time emotions. This technology already exists today. It is far from perfect, but its accuracy is rapidly getting better.

It is already being used:
→ In digital job interviews to measure a candidate's emotions (Hirevue).
→ In classrooms to measure engagement (China).
→ With live audiences to measure audience engagement and emotions (TedX and Teatreneu).

It wil be used soon in:
→ Border security at airports to pick out potentials criminals/terrorists (Avatar).
→ Retail, to measure shopper's emotions and give them a tailormade response (Shelfpoint).
→ Heathcare, to monitor patient's emotions and pain levels (Nvisu).

But what if it could be used in the world of romantic relationships? Tinder 3.0? What if employers could measure employee engagement in real-time at the office or monitor them whilst working from home? And what would this technology do when used in a sales meeting / negotiation? Emotion AI can assess if a person is lying, which means we could have lie detectors all around us. What would that mean?

Sharing the above examples is a great start for a group discussion. If you are the moderator, please explain that with emotion AI, it is not the technical or legal side that will determine how this technology will enter our lives; rather it will be an ethical question: is this what we want? As people? As a society?

When the discussion on emotion AI is over, it is time to bridge the gap to the specific organization. Pick a practical ethical issue and ask the group which arguments from the discussion they just had are applicable to their own ethical dilemma. The group will now automatically start using similar language and argumentation as before. In my experience the conversation is a lot more balanced and constructive than starting this conversation without doing the *other* industry exercise first.

5.4

ETHICS PITFALLS: MORAL LICENSING, PURPOSE WASHING, AND CANCEL CULTURE

Navigating the world of ethical decision making can feel like walking on egg shells... because that's what it is. Unfortunately. If it was as straightforward as doing a profit-loss statement the world would probably be in a different place. Because 'doing the right thing' does not necessarily mean that it is easy, that all ethical initiatives are welcomed by everyone and all outcomes are only positive.

One of the most common human flaws associated with ethical behavior is 'moral licensing'. This means that doing good will give that person a license to do something bad: a permission to sin. "I have run 15k today, so now I'll eat that hamburger and flush it down with a coke." Or, "I don't eat meat, I drive an electric car and have solar panels on my roof, so flying to Milan for a weekend of shopping is fine." An easy way to spot moral licensing behavior is when people use the words 'I deserve'. People subconsciously feel like they deserve a 'reward' for doing something righteous. Even if that reward nullifies their righteous behavior.

The research is overwhelming. From people who are more likely to cheat and steal after they have bought a 'green' product, to people with a strong non-racist self-image who are more likely to unconsciously discriminate against racial minorities. Interestingly, moral licensing can also work the other way around: the bad can proceed the good. "I really deserve this big steak as I'll have a meat-free weekend starting tomorrow."

Moral licensing can also happen in groups, where people start 'compensating' for each other's behavior. This can pose a challenge for organizations. While there is overwhelming research showing that ethical leadership will lead to employees adopting the same behavior, there are also studies that show ethical behavior from leaders can backfire. In some experiments employees are more likely to act in abusive ways after their leaders demonstrate ethical behavior. The research is not conclusive here. But one thing is clear: it is most important to be aware of the moral licensing effect ethical behavior can have, on yourself, friends, family members, and colleagues.

How to deal with moral licensing? Stanford psychologist Kelly McGonigal advises a series of steps. First, recognize it is a deeply human response. In other words, we all do this in one form or another. Secondly, zoom out. Stop focussing on weighing each behavioral action in and of itself. Stop dividing all actions into good or bad, right or wrong categories, because one's rationale will search for a balance. Instead have an end goal in sight and make your actions part of that. Thirdly, make doing the right thing an integral component of your identity.

This last one is also a great piece of advice for organizations, as many do not make ethics part of their identity, but rather 'outsource' it to their marketing communications department. The result is 'Purpose washing', also known as 'Green washing', 'Diversity washing', 'Privacy washing' and more recently, 'Woke washing.' Apologies for the buzzword bingo, but even Unilever's CEO warned against woke-washing and the US Chamber of Commerce calls our times 'the Purpose Zeitgeist'.

Behind the buzzwords is solid (academic) research on the importance of having a purpose as an organization: a more motivated workforce, higher productivity, more growth, and a higher profit. In a global study carried out by PWC,

analysts found that of the companies with a clearly defined purpose, 90% of them deliver growth and profits at or above the industry average. And the motivation of workers spikes in these companies: two-thirds of their work force say they are passionate about their work versus one-third in companies without a clearly defined purpose. A global study by LinkedIn showed that employees work longer for employers with a clear purpose.

Purpose washing, Diversity washing, Privacy washing, Woke washing

When job hunting, young people are actively looking for companies that have ethics in their purpose. In a wonderful study by the university of Chicago, researchers shared two different job ads across various job boards. They were exactly the same, the only difference was that one had a paragraph on the company's ethical purpose. There were three staggering results. Firstly, the 'ethical' job attracted 33% more applicants. Secondly, people who applied for the 'ethical' firm were actually more productive per hour. They were 10% to 25% more productive than the average employee. Lastly, this effect was primarily driven by women in terms of productivity. The researchers concluded that women, more than men, are actively looking for ethical purpose in a job.

But increasingly, organizations formulate a purpose that does not match with reality. That's purpose washing. Take for example Nike. They have a great purpose statement: "Our purpose is to unite the world through sport to create a healthy planet, active communities and an equal playing field for all." But environmental groups who analyse fashion brands report Nike only uses 'some' eco-friendly materials, and implements 'some' water reduction initiatives. Labour rights activists say Nike does not do enough in making sure its workers get a fair wage, only auditing the final stage in production. Or take Blackrock, the largest investment firm in the world. Its CEO, Larry Fink, is famous for writing an annual letter to CEOs around the world. The themes of the past few years have covered long-termism, ESG, and the climate crisis, and contain much on ethical purpose. Fink says CEOs have to think about the society they operate in, take care of their workers, and take care of the environment. A laudable message. But why does Blackrock still invest substantially in oil and coal? It has more than 5% of the shares in ExxonMobil, Shell, Chevron, and Glencore. And why did Blackrock, as a shareholder, vote mostly against environmentally friendly resolutions in shareholder meetings? And how does the fact that Blackrock is the world's largest investor in nuclear weapons align with Larry Fink's message?

Purpose washing is often not crystal clear. Take Shell, the oil company. The optimist in me sees their homepage is filled with ethical content: reducing CO2, whale development, an electric future, climate targets etc. But the pessimist in me deep dives into the numbers and sees that Shell's investments in oil and gas are far greater than in renewables. And yes, Shell is still the fourth biggest polluter in the world. The optimist in me thinks of the activist shareholders and court cases against Shell and how this woke up their leaders (pun intended) to change course. The pessimist in me then remembers what a recruiter here in the Netherlands told me a few years ago. That the main reason Shell talk about the environment so much, is that otherwise talent won't even apply. It is not for their consumers or politicians, they recognize that smart young talent only wants to work for a company with an ethical purpose. Such blurred realities make forming an opinion very challenging.

From a legal perspective green washing – demonstrably employing false environmental claims – is illegal. But it is unfortunately quite easy to cause confusion around an organization's 'ethical' image by making a vague-ish claim like: "New package! Contains 50% less plastic!". Not a false or misleading claim, but it's still very much a plastic package.

From ethics conversations to ethical action - how many more IPCC reports do we need?

To demystify claims like this and debunk purpose washing we need trustworthy sources where ethical (mis)information will be checked. Similar to accountants checking the finances of organizations, we need 'ethical accountants' checking the ethical claims organizations make. Over the past decade, I have worked for three of the 'big four' global accountancy firms and have been advising them to do just that. To think about a future for their business where they would also start to measure and report on the ethical performance of organizations. In other words, it is great to have a purpose, but are you acting upon it as well? This is what the 2020s will be about, moving from ethics conversations to ethical action. We have talked enough about global warming – how many more IPCC reports do we need? It's time for action.

This is also a great way to prevent getting 'canceled'. Most organizations will be familiar with cancel culture: it is the practice of withdrawing support and publicly shaming individuals and companies after they have done something considered objectionable or offensive. When done well, this can be very effective. I often consider these actions as the online equivalent of a street protest where a busy intersection or the entrance to a building gets blocked. Over the past few years cancel culture has unfortunately spread to personal relationships as well, where for example teens 'cancel' each other. Via social media, it is easy to 'cancel' a person. Often there is an ethical argument for doing so: 'she said something racist' or 'he cheated on me'. This ethical argument would justify the action of cancelling. The problem is that in most cancel cases it is a one way street: there is no context, there is no conversation and there is no empathy. You're canceled, bye!

If we, want people to grow, organizations to develop and societies to flourish, we need an empathetic dialogue and not a public shaming culture that's akin to a medieval square. With that said, organizations and their leaders can quite easily become victims of cancel culture as everyone and every organization makes mistakes. The best way to respond is to apologize sincerely, be empathetic and try to keep the conversation open. Indeed, to lead by example.

STRATEGIC TAKEAWAY

Leaders should be aware of the sensitivities and pitfalls when embarking on an ethics journey. The first step is to be aware of one's own and the organization's moral licensing behavior. The second is not to purpose wash. And last but not least, be prepared to be hit by cancel culture.

5.5

PURITANISM FALLACY

It's understandable that skepticism creeps in when faced with so much purpose washing in the world, but I would urge you not to do that. It's a fallacy to think that if a company has an ethical purpose or an ethical marketing campaign that automatically means all of its business and actions should be ethical. I call this the 'puritanism fallacy'. And it's not only applicable to organizations, but also to individuals.

Many teenagers around the world are at the forefront of global climate crisis protests. Yet commentators question their sincerity, as many of these same teens wear fast-fashion clothing, take a low-cost airline for their summer holidays and are not vegetarian. Conclusion: they are not really worried about the climate, they just want a day off from school/university. This kind of reasoning is an emotional defence mechanism. By pointing out contradictions in behavior, then their actions don't have to be taken seriously at all. Only if someone is completely pure in their actions can their message be taken seriously. This is the reason Greta Thunberg has to take a sailing boat if she wants to travel to the other side of the world, because if she'd flown she would have given fuel to her opponents to discredit her message and personally (insincere attention seeker!). Al Gore, who made two documentaries on global warming (*An Inconvenient Truth* and *An Inconvenient Sequel*) has been widely criticized and called a hypocrite for having a large home and consuming a lot more (green) energy than the average American household. In the Netherlands the climate strike teenagers

were criticized for being hypocrites. The reason? After the climate strike street protests not everyone had cleaned up their mess.

If we want positive change in the world and more ethics in decision making we need to let go of this utopian quest for puritanism. Nobody is perfect and no organization is perfect. It is easy to criticise ethical actions from large multinationals like Shell, Nike, and Blackrock. Just as I have in these very pages. But I could also have expressed appreciation while asking for more: "Great start. Now let's see if you can do X, Y, and Z as well."

Great start! Now let's do X, Y, and Z as well

We should take the same approach with people. Around the globe, politicians who rally for ethics in political decision making are often confronted by critics who will respond with "but in 2015 you said this!" or "in 2012 you voted the other way!" With this omnipresent negative response, politicians are cautious about changing their minds and advocating ethical policies. To quote one of my heroes, stand-up comedian and corporate speaker Deborah Frances-White: "All comedians said things ten years ago we wouldn't say now because society's made progress, and engaged comedians reflect or even help shape

that. There's language we all use now that'll seem clumsy or even offensive in ten years' time. Progress means NOW will be problematic THEN."

I'd encourage everybody to take the long-term view. It might seem to be baby steps now, but in ten years time, it's these steps that can make a difference. In an interview in 2016 about his legacy as a president, Barack Obama said: "Sometimes the task of government is to make incremental improvements or try to steer the ocean liner two degrees north or south so that, ten years from now, suddenly we're in a very different place than we were. At the moment, people may feel like we need a fifty-degree turn; we don't need a two-degree turn. And you say, 'Well, if I turn fifty degrees, the whole ship turns (capsizes)'." Generally speaking this is true, but some of the challenges we are facing do need more than a two-degree turn: the climate crisis for example. And the fast global response to the Covid pandemic showed we can if we all rally behind the same goal with everything we have.

STRATEGIC TAKEAWAY

Often, the media and the general public will criticize leaders and organizations who have started on an ethics journey for not being 100% ethical in everything they do or did in the past. It's an unattainable quest for moral puritanism that is slowing action down. Leaders can respond with: "nobody is perfect, this is the first step and yes, we are going to do more."

5.6

INDIRECT ACTIVISM & NUDGE THE NUDGERS

In the spirit of puritanism, and as this is the last section, I'd like to share my own purpose and the ethics of my company, WHETSTON. It's easy to analyze the actions of others, but what if I look in the mirror and share my own personal take on ethics? One of the core values of Whetston is indirect activism.

Classic activists are seldom invited into boardrooms or strategic off-sites. They are considered too confrontational as often activists want radical changes (like abolishing that very board). Whetston's expertise stems from the belief that 'the future of human behavior' is considered a friendly and safe topic that everyone warmly welcomes.

But as I talk about what drives humans, their needs, their wants, I automatically speak on what is fundamentally best for people in general, whether they are clients, colleagues or other stakeholders. And that is quite simply a healthy planet, a safe and equal society, and fulfilling work with a purpose that not only leads to personal but also societal well-being. If orga-

nizations and leaders want of all of this, their strategy has to be an ethical one, *they have to do the right thing.*

And although deep-diving into human behavior inherently leads to ethics, it does not mean I can approach ethics head on. At Whetston we've had a special keynote on ethics since 2017, but we've been able to convince clients to put this topic on the agenda only a handful of times. Just the word 'ethics' in the title of a keynote or leadership workshop is too confrontational, too activist.

We've therefore been 'hiding' ethics as a subtopic in other presentations and workshops. Whether it's topics like the Trust Transition, Human Adaptation of New Technology, or Generation Z, ethics is woven in there. We never start with ethics, it's always addressed somewhere in the middle. In that way the topic lands with ease. In fact, we often hear afterwards that people were very glad we touched upon the topic of ethics and that we made it tangible and practical in a non-confrontational way.

Over the years, I have been advising this indirect activist strategy to leaders: don't let your marketing department 'hijack' ethics and scream it too loud from the rooftops, but approach it with care and 'indirectism'. And don't be disappointed if an ethical challenge can't be solved overnight: sometimes baby steps are exactly what's required. I like to echo the ocean liner analogy from Barack Obama: a small nudge on the ship's wheel can make a huge change over time.

Future proof leaders have to step up and steer their ocean liner in the right direction

Last but not least, we try to nudge the nudgers. In other words, get leaders to change their views so they will start to change the views of their people, customers and stakeholders.

There is nothing more satisfying than nudging a decision-maker towards doing the right thing. It is very important to acknowledge this is impossible without bottom-up grassroots activism. Because societal change most often starts there and people researchers like myself use these movements in our analyses to convince the boardroom to change.

For all the leaders, please realize that just thinking about ethics and embedding this in a long term strategy is a privilege: you are at the steering wheel of change! In presentations I often use the example of Emmanuel Macron, the French president, in conversation with a 'yellow vest' street protester. The protester was enraged by Macron's new environmental policies: "Mr. President, you are worried about the end of the century, I am worried about the end of the month!" If you're worrying about how to pay the bills this month and feed your family, it's very hard to consider the greater good in the long term. Dear leaders, because you have the privilege of not having to worry about the end of the month, you have a moral obligation to steer the liner in the right direction.

And part of that right direction is also increasing income and wealth equality, which was one of the main drivers of the yellow vest protests. Let's side step and take a look at two developments. Firstly the historical analysis of the wage ratio (the ratio of the executive salaries in an organization compared to the average worker) shows that from the 1980's onwards, executive pay has exploded. For example, the US went from 40 – 1 to 265 – 1 in 2018. Around the globe, we see similar numbers. The current ratios are countries like the UK (201 – 1), India (229 – 1) and South Africa (180 – 1). Secondly is the global development of wealth distribution, where the inequality is even greater compared to income inquality. Currently, the world's richest 1% have *twice* as much wealth as 6.8 billion people combined.

You are worried about the end of the century, I am worried about the end of the month!

Globally, both the income and wealth gap still keep getting bigger. During the 2020's this trend needs to get reversed if we want to decrease social unrest and reach a bigger acceptance of green policies. It's for future proof leaders to step up and steer their ocean liner in the right direction.

Decision makers should realize they are in the privileged position of being able to worry about the long-term future and therefore have the moral obligation to do the right thing. It is not complicated: if we want the best for ourselves, human beings, that automatically means a healthy planet, a safe and equal society, and fulfilling work with a purpose that not only leads to personal, but also societal well-being. That is great for any organization.

6.
MENTAL SURPLUS

6.1 The normalizing of mental health
6.2 Gen Z: anxious activists
6.3 Mental health & technology
6.4 Suffering from home
6.5 Creating a mental surplus

In the late 1990s, I was in my early twenties and enjoying student life at Maastricht University. When I consider health issues at that time, I can only remember sport injuries and a fear of RSI (repetitive strain injury), which was a topical ailment then. But there was little discussion of mental health or problems such as anxiety, stress, or sleeping disorders. Mental health awareness at the university was minimal – there were no university psychologists, coaches, or counselors. In my final year, my mom was diagnosed with a terminal illness and I postponed writing my Master's thesis. I wrote a letter to the faculty board explaining the situation, asking for a study delay. The response was a swift and practical 'take the time you need' – nothing less, but also nothing more.

In the twenty years that have passed since then, awareness of mental health and mental well-being has shifted fundamentally. Not only is it increasingly a topic that can be discussed openly, but a practical mental health infrastructure is rapidly being rolled out across society, and particularly in education. In 2018, in an effort to combat exam anxiety, the University of Amsterdam created a 'puppy room' – literally a room full of puppies that students could stroke, cuddle, and interact with, helping reduce stress. With limited places and 15-minute time slots it was immediately oversubscribed.[1] Since 2015, the UK has had an annual Children's Mental Health Week, to "shine a spotlight on the importance of children and young people's mental health" with a focus on education.[2]

In 2015, the UN added 'mental health' to its Sustainable Development Goals (SDGs), and defined mental health as "a priority for global development for the next 15 years."[3] Around that time, sociologists increasingly reported teens and twenty-somethings suffering from depression, stress and anxiety.[4][5] For example, universities in the UK saw a fivefold increase in the number of students disclosing mental health conditions from 2007 to 2017.[6]

By the end of the 2010s, organizations and their leaders were starting to wake up to the fact that mental health was as important a work issue as a healthy lunch or a supportive office chair. In 2019, the WHO estimated that 25% of adults would be affected by work-related burnout at some point in their active life, defining it as "chronic workplace stress that has not been successfully managed" and which leads to "reduced professional efficacy".[7]

Enter Covid and the acceleration increased. Stress, anxieties, burnouts, suicidal thoughts, sleeping disorders: the numbers exploded. On average, all indicators doubled. Meaning twice as many people reported stress, and twice as many people took anti-depressants.[8 9 10 11]

The flipside of this alarming development is that many of the leaders I work with are now waking up to this development.[12] In a 2021 study from Boston University 200 HR leaders were asked about their top priorities. Their number 1 answer: 'employee well-being and mental health.'[13] Leaders are realizing mental health is as vital as physical health.

I believe this is just the beginning. The 2020s will prove to be a pivotal decade when it comes to recognising and responding to mental health challenges and that future proof leaders will include the creation of a 'mental surplus' in their future strategies.

This means simply that organizations and individuals need to proactively invest in mental health on a regular basis even if there seems to be no need. It is buying an ergonomic desk before the back problems begin – not after. It is regular car maintenance to avoid being stranded on a busy highway. This shift is already happening, especially among younger people as they approach mental health differently from their older counterparts.

6.1
THE NORMALIZING OF MENTAL HEALTH

When the Covid pandemic hit the world, it was immediately seen by the media and the gurus on LinkedIn as an accelerator of digital trends, particularly remote or hybrid working, cloud computing, and e-health. But less conspicuously there was a more important development: the acceleration of the normalization of mental health.

The 20th century saw a wake up call with regard to physical health and there were two key outcomes: a focus on exercising regularly and on eating healthily. At the start of the century, sports and exercise not related to labor were of little interest to the general public. The Olympic Games was in its infancy, and physical exercise classes in schools were only just appearing. World War II was a turning point. Physically fit soldiers were needed, yet in a lot of countries many were not healthy enough. For example, in the US, 45% of the first two million men drafted into the army failed their physicals. It put physical education on the radar and a nationwide program was rolled out in American schools.[14]

With the progress of medical science in the second half of the 20th century, governments started to increasingly influence healthy eating and living. This saw the growth of anti-smoking awareness (global smoking rates cut in half from 1950 – 2000[15]) as well as the UN developing programs for under- and over-nutrition. By the 21st century, the importance of exercising regularly and eating well was a given. Quite a percentage of the world population do not act upon it or they do not have access to affordable healthy food, but the awareness is there. And sports are now for everyone, not just for the elite or a group of obsessive early adopters.

The same dynamic is now happening in mental health. Is it rapidly becoming a given as well. Take professional sports. Twenty years ago the perception was that an athlete would only visit

own professional institutions and associations. It is expected over the next decade that more and more of these mental health work fields will be included in the academic realm and legal restrictions, licensing, and regulation will be more rigorously developed.

Imagine that in ten years from now you not only have a gym membership, but also a mental gym membership. The first mental health gyms are already here. For example COA, a mental gym founded in 2021, offers all kinds of classes, like emotional fit leadership. Their claim is that "Your emotional fitness is as important as your physical fitness".[16] While COA targets knowledge workers, the shift to all layers of society has begun. In the Netherlands, former plumber Hans Andriessen has founded Bouwmind ('bouw' is Dutch for 'constructing') and he offers mental health coaching for construction workers. He states that these workers need mental help at least as much as knowledge workers because a construction site is a physically hazardous place where one has to be constantly alert. Work culture is to never complain and that all problems have a practical solution. Andriessen has observed construction workers are happy to work positively on their mental health, but only if is not done overtly and avoids 'obvious' terminology such as meditation or mindfulness.

Construction workers embrace developing their mental health

a mental health coach if there was something wrong with them. Now all professional athletes will focus on mental health as a key facet of their training and performance.

Many coaches (and counsellors and therapists) deliver mental health services that traditional psychiatrists and clinical psychologists won't or cannot. Coaches are filling the gaps in the mental health spectrum. The whole 'industry' is still very much under construction. Many mental health professionals are accredited by their

Organizations must perceive mental health to be as vital as physical health. It is vitally important not simply for knowledge workers, but for every employee or citizen.

6.2

GEN Z: ANXIOUS ACTIVISTS

The biggest leap forward for mental health will stem from a generational shift. The way Generation Z (those born after 1998) approach mental health is revelatory to those of us approaching middle-age. When I have a drink with my male friends – who are all in their forties – and I share with them that I hurt my elbow riding my mountain bike, a lively conversation starts. War stories are shared about sporting injuries, different treatments are discussed and everyone has the contact details of a specialist or two that can help me. Now compare this to the following scenario: I decide to share a mental injury with them. I haven't been sleeping well lately, because I am anxious and stressed. There will be a silence, one or two questions, a pat on the back and then the advice to have another drink or take a day off. If this sounds all too familiar, you're probably my age.

The Gen Z approach to this would be completely different. The media rather derogatorily called them the 'depressed generation" even before the pressures of the pandemic. Gen Z mental health statistics have alarmed many. When Covid hit, youngsters in their teens and twenties suffered the most compared to older generations. In a global study (45 countries) in 2021, 46% of Gen Z stated they feel stressed all or most of the time.[17] In the United States, the figures are even more alarming. In 2020, in a large study carried out by the Centers for Disease Control and Prevention in the US, researchers found that 63% of 18 to 24 year olds reported experiencing anxiety and depression, with a quarter of young adults reporting that they had considered suicide in the past thirty days.[18] These numbers are more than double those for my own age group, Generation X.[19]

Experts are debating whether Gen Z genuinely suffers more mental health issues, or if, as a generation, they are simply far more open about discussing and improving it. This is the generation that grew up in the wake of the economic crisis of 2007/2008; learned about the climate crisis through a series of ever-more-alarming reports; became educated in the light cast by the #metoo and BLM (Black Lives Matter) movements; understood and raised awareness of increasing inequality; and then – to top it all off – Covid impacted their formative years.[20] But while the older generations mostly pushed their sorrows away, Gen Z embraces mental health with an awe-inspiring openness that I hope to have one day myself.

I have four younger colleagues and the ease they have with discussing mental health is impressive

During the pandemic it is not Covid Gen Z has been most concerned about. While 'old' people immediately put Covid top of our concerns list, young people started worrying about the climate even more. During the pandemic I had a conversation with a group of my students who were very frustrated that the pandemic saw world leaders free up huge budgets and act instantaneously, while climate action policies continued to be actioned over decades. Multiple studies have shown young people are increasingly worried and anxious about global warming and many suffer from so-called climate anxiety.[21] In a large global study among 18–25 year olds published in Nature in 2021, 60% said they felt 'very worried' or 'extremely worried' about global warming, and the vast majority feel governments are not nearly doing enough. Although some media frame this as a 'Western' phenomenon, it absolutely is not. The countries with the highest proportion of respondents who felt 'very worried' or 'extremely worried' by climate change were the Philippines (84%), India (68%) and Brazil (67%). These are countries where the impact of climate change has been hard-hitting for years.[22]

Fortunately their premature world weariness does not lead to inertia. The response from Gen Z is two-fold. The first is that their anxiousness, anger, and frustration leads to activism. Gen Z pushed the soft 'clicktivism' from the early 2010s – online campaigning through shares and likes – towards the radical cancel culture we discussed in the previous chapter. They fired up old-fashioned physical street activism, with Greta Thunberg's climate strike at the forefront. There have also been teenage strikes in Italy protesting schools opening during the Covid lockdowns, and in the Netherlands in a push for better mental health care.

When it comes to mental health this generation is also the most active in seeking professional help. Twice as many of them have accessed professional help compared to the babyboomer generation.[23] Seeking help can also take other forms. For example, there is a growing trend of (virtual) climate cafés around the world, where young people gather not so much to plan action, but rather have a free and safe space to discuss their climate anxiety.[24]

They are open to talking about their mental health problems and the best treatments. I have four younger colleagues and the ease they have with discussing mental health is impressive. They have all seen psychologists, coaches, or therapists and continue to do so as they deem fit. I have tried – and continue to try – to learn from them and adopt their active approach to mental health.

The advice I have for leaders is to do the same. Do not pick up the mental health baton with a group of peers but have Generation Z help you out. In effect, reverse mentoring on mental health. Many organizations have reverse mentoring programs in place, but mostly in tech and digital. Take the enthusiasm you showed when your intern finally showed you how to start a TikTok account and apply it to your organization's mental health challenges. I guarantee you will learn something. I've worked with several leaders recently who were successful in finding a great reverse Gen Z mentor and their

experience was unequivocally positive. One of the leaders, a partner at global law firm, reported back to us that he received the best leadership advice in years. If the hierarchical culture of your organization impedes this - sometimes junior colleagues may not feel comfortable speaking freely to senior management – then talk to individuals or groups outside the business.

STRATEGIC TAKEAWAY

Gen Z is the generation that reports the most mental health problems, but also discusses mental health with the most ease. Leaders should take note and have these youngsters reverse mentor them on mental health. It is often best to find a reverse mentor outside one's own organization as they will feel more open to respond with honesty and frankness.

The countries with the highest proportion
of respondents who felt 'very worried'
or 'extremely worried' by climate change
were the Philippines, India, and Brazil

6.3
MENTAL HEALTH & TECHNOLOGY

In Chapter 4 we explored the challenge of finding a sane digital balance in our relationships, at work, and within a business strategy. We all know that too much screen time and digital device overload has potentially negative effects on our well-being. But when a new device or technology is introduced, how do we safely gauge its impact on our mental health? Ideally it is tested extensively first in real life situations, by objective research groups in different geographies who share and build on each others' research. Yet the reality sees technological developments launched into the market as swiftly as possible and 'first mover advantage' dominates the world of ICT. Facebook's old internal motto was 'Move fast, break things' which they abandoned in 2014 after, you guessed it, breaking too many things and too many people.

It is us, the citizens, consumers, and users who are the crash test dummies of modern technology. From a mental health perspective, the Millennials (those born between 1980 and the late 90s) were the true guinea pigs for the smartphone and social media. Of course all generations had access to the technology at the same time, but it was the Millennial generation who started to use it in their adolescence (when one is most focussed on their peers and the outside world). Regrettably there was little to no guidance for adolescent users, because

this technology was also brand new to parents, teachers, and legislators. As noted previously, it often takes 15 years for a technology to 'land' in society, and even longer to land in the world of education.

Young people are very vulnerable during their adolescence, and with little to no supervision and incorrect use, social media can be devastating. One of the most shocking studies I have come across is from the United States, which looked at suicides amongst teenage girls. The numbers were steady until the introduction of social media and platforms such as Facebook and Instagram. In the first ten years after their introduction there was a 70% increase in suicide amongst females aged 15–19 and a 151% increase in the 10–14 age group.[25] Researchers are reluctant to conclude that social media are the only cause of this trend, but even Meta (that runs Facebook and Instagram) conceded that social media has a toxic effect on mental health.[26]

Millennials had to navigate the development and growing prevalence of fake news, online dating, sexting, managing online identities, cyberbullying and digital addiction without support. Yes, my generation (Gen X) had to do that as well, but we knew we could always fall back on our tried and tested analog lifestyles.

I didn't have a mobile phone (the precursor to the smartphone) until my last year at university, and even then I only used it for calls and a few text messages per month. I did also receive a university email account, though I can't remember emailing anyone with it!

The Millennial generation were the true guinea pigs for the smartphone and social media

Generation Z (who come after the Millennials) reaped the benefits: they are increasingly privacy aware, learned from the social media mistakes of the Millennials, and their parents and teachers were now tech savvy enough to guide them through a digital society. In the late 2010s legislation finally started to catch up with the rampant fake news polluting social media platforms. To many they were still only baby steps, but if we zoom out and take a long term perspective, it's important to note that social media and smartphones are, in relative terms, still in their infancy.

Here is a great rule of thumb when in doubt about a new technology: take a look at how the designers of the technology are using it. Many Millennial employees from the ICT sector have recognized the adverse effects social media and the smartphone have had on their mental well being, with movements such as Time Well Spent and Design for Happiness trying to force the tech giants to make mental well-being a priority. The Centre for Humane Technology (which came out of the Time Well Spent movement) distinguishes six main negative effects from social media usage in its current form:[27]

#1 – Making the Trivial Seem Urgent
Notifications constantly trigger us, but most of the time these are false alarms, compromising our ability to attend to what is important.

#2 – Encouraging Seeking Without Fulfilment
Technology often capitalizes on the potency of wanting, providing endless possibilities for seeking but few experiences that give enduring satisfaction.

#3 – Forcing Us to Multitask
Social media inspires multitasking, which is associated with poorer memory, increased impulsivity, and changes in brain function.

#4 – Weaponizing Fear and Anxiety
Social media content that generates fear, anger and disgust propels deeper engagement and spreads much faster than positive content. It can erode our sense of goodness and our shared humanity.

#5 – Encouraging Constant Social Comparison
Measuring ourselves against others commonly leads to negative emotions: envy, shame, anxiety, conceit. It can lead to compulsive comparison, self-doubt, and egocentric melodrama.

#6 – Telling Us Whatever We Want to Believe
Software algorithms learn about our preferences and customize the information we receive. We celebrate supportive information and dismiss contradictory information. Taken to an extreme, we become more polarized and lose a sense of ourselves as a cohesive social group.

These six negative effects are rooted in (academic) research and valid concerns. But they are also part of the societal adaptation process any new technology will go through. The 2010s can be seen as the wild years of experimentation and unleashing the smartphone and social media on the masses. In the 2020s these technologies will slowly land, and we'll see regulation and legislation, new social norms, and experienced users who will use social media more as a tool and less of a replacement for human contact. Columbia professor John Cacioppo, an expert on loneliness, says doing just that can make your life better: "If you use Facebook to organise face-to-face contact, it increases your social capital." So if you use social media to plan to go to a concert with friends, that is great for your mental health. If you turn to social media instead of meeting friends and going to a concert, that has a reverse effect.[28]

As discussed in Chapter 4, there is room for a new wave of social media, the development of platforms that make us more happy and improve our relationships, instead of platforms that just try to lock us in for as long as possible in any way they can. These new platforms would not have us compete with each other in a winner takes all race for the most likes. I truly believe that the next Facebook will be a social medium that fundamentally improves our mental health – the technology, data, and attitudes make this possible and feasible.

The next Facebook will be a social medium that fundamentally improves our mental health

Societal pressure led many tech companies in the late 2010s to launch initiatives to help their users employ their products and services in a more mentally healthy way – for example, Google's Digital Well-being tools or Facebook's 'quiet mode'. But these features are akin to alcohol companies that promote 'drink responsibly' or sports car brands like Porsche telling their customers to obey the speed limit.

Interestingly, tech companies engage significant resources in measuring eyeballs, clicks, and engagement of everything we do online. Wouldn't it be great if they could shift that focus to measuring our mental well-being and then increasing it? And I don't mean the current 'review culture' we are in, where we are asked to review every tiny online interaction. As the goal of these reviews is not to make the user or the consumer happier, but to sell more, or – at the very least – improve the product for future consumer use and adoption.

STRATEGIC TAKEAWAY

The gung-ho, guinea pig years of social media are over. Tech firms will increasingly (be forced to) adapt their products and services to improve our mental health and not erode it. Future proof leaders should ask themselves: if we want to win tomorrow, how can we start to improve the mental well-being of our users / customers today?

6.4

SUFFERING FROM HOME

If there was one work-related question during the Covid pandemic I received most, it was on working from home (WFH) and remote working. How much WFH should office workers do? What is the best remote-office balance? How do individuals and organizations maximise productivity, creativity, and mental health in the post-Covid world?

The global lockdown forced many to work from home and gave researchers access to amounts of real data no normal WFH study could. The data itself is conclusive: too much WFH/remote work can be disastrous for many people – they are less productive, less creative/innovative and their mental health declines.[29]

Of key concern, is that remote working sees engagement levels between people decline sharply. There are two main reasons for this. Firstly, the seemingly trivial yet socially vital watercooler moments are lost in the world of the virtual office. It's those conversations that build relationships and team dynamics, not during a powerpoint slideshow or the discussion of Q3 figures. Secondly, it is very hard for people to engage via a screen. Most of our body language gets lost because there is no eye contact, most people only film their head (and do not include their upper body) and mirroring one another – which subconsciously boosts engagement – does not work virtually. This has a dev-

astating effect on individual relationships, but also damaging effects on teamwork.[30] People in several WFH studies report feeling they are only a 'worker' and not part of a team.

A number of older leaders told me during the pandemic they were feeling engaged with their peers and questioned the (academic) research. Yet many of these leaders had been working together with their colleagues for years, sometimes decades. These long-term work relationships can endure a significant period of working from home before disengagement kicks in. It's not a surprise that it was mostly the younger employees and the new hires who were suffering the most from a lack of engagement whilst WFH.

In the first year of the pandemic, the reports that showed a boost in productivity were prevalent, but in the second year the balance tipped the other way. Ultimately, the decreased engagement impacted on most workers and this affected productivity and creativity. Some studies showed productivity was still up from pre-Covid times, but this was mainly caused by workers putting in more hours.[31] Later studies are all based on a fully WFH pandemic situation compared to pre-pandemic figures.

The best solution with regard to our mental health is one of the buzzwords of the early

The physically present people
will engage automatically
and effectively

2020s: hybrid. And the million-dollar-question is what the most effective remote vs. physical work ratio will be. My answer is quite simple. If we take a classic five-day work week, three or four days are in the office and one or two days can be based at home. These one or two days should be used for deep work: tasks that require concentration with no distractions. Dialing-in from home into a meeting with colleagues who are physically at the office might be technically possible, but is not advisable from an engagement perspective. The physically-present people will engage automatically and effectively while the remote colleagues will be literally – but also emotionally – distant.

Bricks-and-mortar companies may have to close: convert them to small, remote work hubs

Some organizations use buddy systems where a physical colleague is responsible for supporting a remote colleague in a meeting, which does lead to marginal engagement gains.[32] My advice to clients is to have either a fully physical meeting or a fully virtual meeting. This creates a level playing field for all colleagues. Some tech experts predict that during this decade we will begin meeting in VR environments, like Facebook's Horizon Workrooms. I have yet to see avatars that overcome the 'uncanny valley' problem: avatars that try to look like real people can be very disturbing. So even the most high-tech VR solutions work with cartoon-like avatars – a graphic alter ego – which are hard to engage with exactly because they are not real people.

Why would people choose to spend more time in the office rather than work at home? Why is one or two days at the office not enough? Because if we spend such little time at the office, the pressure on that time will be enormous: to be social, to brainstorm and create, to complete admin, and cram in all the necessary meetings. There will be no time to be human. To take small moments of time to chat with colleagues, to connect, to think. Additionally, for the good of our mental well-being we need separate spaces for our work and our private lives. And believe it or not we benefit from a commute. What commute time do you think is the most advantageous for one's mental health? The answer is 20 minutes, by foot, car, cycle or public transport.[33] From my own research, people working at home told me they needed to mentally switch from private to work mode and went for a walk or bike ride in the morning, or they did some groceries or took the kids to school. But only a fraction did the same at the end of the day. The routine then became 'I am zoomed out', so close the laptop, walk downstairs and crash on the couch. This 30 seconds between the last virtual meeting of the day and 'arriving home' after a hard work day are not enough of a commute and added to the mental stress and fatigue so many people suffered during the pandemic.

Have either a fully physical meeting OR a fully virtual meeting

I've been advising this balance – around 75–80% at the office and 20–25% WFH – to most of my clients for a long time. But this has been a tough piece of advice to follow for many organizations – especially during the pandemic. The reason for that: most organizations asked their workers how much WFH they would like after the pandemic. The results varied quite a bit, but the average answer was a 50/50 split. The exception was in IT/tech, where employees indicated they'd prefer most of their work to be home-based. I strongly disagree with using these results as a rationale for a future HR strategy for two reasons.

1. People do not necessarily know what's best for them. It's like asking a kid how much candy they would like to eat. We know the answer is not going to be a healthy one.

2. One should never ask people in the midst of a crisis situation what they would like after the crisis is over. When in a crisis people tend to overestimate the effect that crisis will have long-term. Again and again we are surprised when post-crisis, most or all aspects of life return to normal. Additionally, the Covid crisis created mental stress and anxiety, which naturally would influence employees, answers. When society began opening up after the first extended lockdowns, many people were initially anxious to be in a social environment again. Office workers reported 'getting back to the office' anxiety.[34] Young people reported party and festival anxiety.[35] Leaders had and still have to realize people sometimes do not know what is best for them. To complicate matters, leaders have faced the same issues as their colleagues, suffering from similar social anxieties.

The early 2020s will no doubt see extensive experimentation as organizations and individuals attempt the find the optimum home/office balance for mental well-being, productivity and creativity.

One potential 'best of both worlds' solution is to remote work from a hub. In large cities like London, many workers have a round trip commute of two hours or more. In a a hub model, an organization could set up small local hubs. So for example in Croydon in the south of

London, there would be a small office space where colleagues can work and meet a few days a week. This combines the short commute and the better work/life balance of WFH with engaging in person with colleagues (as we did in the pre-pandemic office environment). Ideally a hub would have state-of-the-art AV meeting rooms set up to connect with the other hubs and the head office. The challenge of course is in how to organize this, because finding a balance between the office and WFH is a difficult one and with this solution a third space is added to a company's responsibilities. Fortunately there are specialized vendors who offer flexible hub solutions so organizations can begin experimenting with new work strategies almost immediately.

Additionally, as e-commerce and digital solutions will continue growing this decade, it might be the ideal solution for cash-poor bricks-and-mortar companies – the move to small remote work hubs is cost efficient and practical.

STRATEGIC TAKEAWAY

Too much remote work for too long leads to employee engagement levels plummeting, which affects productivity, creativity and mental health. Most people – and therefore most organizations – will fare best with their employees together at an office (HQ or a hub) the majority of the time.

RELATIONSHIP BOOSTER

There is a direct causation between happiness at work and good relationships with colleagues. It is actually one of the best antidotes against work burnout. But how to improve relationships at work? There are book shelves – no, entire libraries – full of books on this subject, but I will share my favorite relationship booster exercise with you. It has worked like magic in many workshops I have run.

This exercise comes from the British philosopher and School of Life founder Alain de Botton.[36] It is based on the premise that in the best relationships, people dare to be vulnerable. In many work cultures, sharing vulnerabilities can be seen as weakness and therefore only successes get shared – even if failing is embraced as part of the innovation process. Luckily, vulnerable leadership has been gaining popularity over the last decade.

To begin, divide the group into pairs – they should decide who is person A and who is person B. If possible, these pairs should not be colleagues that know each other well. The exercise is to answer the following three questions in turn. Person A has 5 minutes to answer, while person B just listens. Then the roles are reversed: person B has 5 minutes to answer the questions and person A just listens.

The three questions are as follows:

1. What are you afraid of?
2. What do you regret?
3. What are you ashamed of?

The meeting leader should emphasize that everyone can decide for themselves how personal they would like to get. For example, you might simply answer that you are afraid of spiders, regret not applying to your current organization straight after college, and are ashamed of your favorite football club losing their last match.

Interestingly, most people don't do that. The first time I did this exercise myself – at the School of Life in Amsterdam – I was matched up with a 25-year-old Spanish girl who was an expat. I did not know her. She went first and she shared

with me that she was afraid she would never find out what she truly wanted to do with her life; she regretted not saying goodbye to her father on his death bed; and she was ashamed of telling her friends and family back in Spain that she was unhappy in Amsterdam, just quit her job and was now working in a coffee shop.

Wow … I was blown out of my seat and when it was my turn it was impossible not to share vulnerabilities at a similar emotional level. When the exercise was over I felt we had more of a bond then I have with some people I have known for years. Although this happened a few years ago, if we met today, I am positive we could pick up our exercise conversation instantly.

To finish the exercise, encourage the pairs to continue their conversation over lunch/coffee/dinner at a later date, if they feel like it. In my experience, most people do. This exercise has been effective in in quite a few workshops and leadership programs over the years. It is often the one exercise people refer back to, even months or years later. And as a bonus, it is a great conversation starter to take home and do with friends and/or family members as well.

6.5

CREATING A MENTAL SURPLUS

The traditional way we have been treating mental well-being at work is coming to an end. By that, I mean that most people only visit a psychologist, psychiatrist, mental coach, or counsellor when they become so ill that they cannot work, sleep, or just simply function anymore. Only then do they receive treatment and are often put back in the same environment or situation that made them ill initially. This is comparable to avoiding exercise and eating candy and French fries for years, and when we get a heart attack returning immediately to our old habits after surgery. When it comes to our physical well-being we exercise and eat healthily to prevent getting a heart attack. We are proactive instead of reactive.

This proactive approach is the essence of what I call *Mental Surplus*. This is being so mentally healthy that even if something terrible happens, like a prolonged stressful situation at work, a divorce or a pandemic, a person has a surplus of mental energy to not fall through the mental ice, and suffer burnout, anxiety, or depression. To use another physical metaphor, the heaviest lifting I need to do on a regular basis is lift up my young kids or put my hand luggage in an overhead compartment in an airplane. But I am physically strong enough to carry a fridge up a flight of stairs. I rarely need to do that, but if necessary, my body could carry that load because I've prepared it to be strong.

In order to create mental surplus one needs to proactively invest in mental health on a regular basis even if there seems to be no need. It is relationship therapy before there is a crisis.[37] It is regular car maintenance before being stranded on a busy highway. It is buying an ergonomic desk before the back problems begin – not after. This shift is already happening, especially among younger people as they approach mental health differently from their older counterparts.

So what is needed for this mental surplus? Here are a few of my favorite pointers. Mind you, these are just a start:

1. EMPATHY

Empathy is a skill that is vital to any high quality relationship. It improves communication and co-operation. People with empathetic leaders report better mental health than those who have leaders who are not empathetic.[38] People around you benefit from it, but it is also proven to be beneficial to reduce one's own stress and prevent burnout. Yes, research has shown that the higher a person's empathy skills, the lower their chances of job burnout.[39] During the 2010s, empathy as a leadership skill gained popularity, especially as more and more hard data proved that it can improve business success.[40] As an example, in a US study, of the people who reported that their leaders were empathetic,

61% of them were able to be innovative at work, compared to only 13% of employees with less empathetic leaders.

Empathy is a win-win with many positive outcomes, but what exactly is it? In working with leaders, I often run into people who confuse empathy with sympathy. The definition of empathy is 'demonstrating an accurate, non-judgmental understanding of the other side's needs, issues and perspectives'.[41] So one does not have to agree with the other side or feel what the other is feeling – the latter is sympathy.[42] It is perfectly possible to be empathetic towards your worst enemy. It's about simply showing that you understand the other. And the good news is that this is a skill that can be taught and learned.

2. LETTING GO OF PERFECTION

This century, the quest for perfection has been taken to extremes never seen before in human history. Take our romantic relationships. Psychotherapist Esther Perel is famous for her analysis that modern relationships have to fulfil the same role a whole village used to provide. Meaning that a partner now not only has to be someone to share a household with and raise children with, but also a person who is a great lover, who gives you social status, who provides great conversation, and – more pressure here – is a true soulmate, for eternity. Perel has observed that the younger people are, the more often they use the word 'perfect'. Modern dating apps offer thousands of potential matches only one click away, adding to the feeling that the perfect partner is out there. The job market is not much different. While the majority of the world population works mainly to feed themselves and their loved ones, in developed countries, a job has to match one's purpose and values, have social status, offer growth options, be dynamic, have fun colleagues, offer the best of international travel and working from home etc. Again, that perfect job must be out there.

Let's say you work in marketing and live in Paris. A simple job search for marketing jobs in the Paris area offers no less than 41,403 results on LinkedIn.

Social media bombards us with impressive careers, glamorous vacations, and perfect relationships. Although we rationally understand social media is not a one-on-one portrayal of reality, subconsciously we believe perfection is also attainable for us. And the online influencers, gurus, and 'experts' tell us that yes! this perfection is indeed achievable. If, of course, their advice is followed.

The younger people are, the more often they use the word 'perfect'

In a large-scale meta-analysis involving 77 studies on perfection, researchers found that perfectionism has increased substantially over the past 25 years and that "young people are drowning in the rising tide of perfectionism."[44] Recent psychological research shows that the happiest people with the least burnouts are the ones who are not on a quest for perfection. This means that to maximise happiness, one has to let go of maximising and settle for 'good enough'.[45]

This goes against much of the modern business wisdom where we all should strive for the best organization, the best products, the best service and our best selves. 'The best' is a fallacy. Let me compare it to buying a pair of new jeans. When I was young I lived in a small town with a handful of clothing stores. If I needed a new pair of jeans as a teenager, I visited all these stores, tried on the three or four pairs of jeans that were my size and budget and then bought the least bad one and never had a second thought about them. Now I buy my jeans online. As an example, Amazon's male fashion department offers me 5000+ results. That means the perfect pair is out there and if if I buy a pair and my jeans do not fit and look perfect, it's my own fault. I should have searched better, further, and more carefully.

There is no easy fix here. One simple exercise perfectionists can take is to practice letting go of perfection in an everyday situation. Example: when in a supermarket, just pick a queue without thinking and stay there. Instead of being a perfectionist and first calculating which queue is really the longest by analysing the number of items people have in their carts. And second, scan the faces and body language of the different cashiers to determine who works fastest. Being a (former) perfectionist myself, I will admit I used to do all of that.

3. DAWDLE

Closely linked to the search for perfection is the maximizing of one's work day and filling every (billable) minute with back-to-back meetings and completing one's to-do list. The key to mental surplus is to not work at one's full capacity and also build in 'dawdle' time.

Over the past few years I have heard quite a few CEOs address their people and try to motivate them. More often than not, maximizing was part of their message. A few years ago the CEO of one of my clients, an IT multinational, encouraged his people at a leadership event (with the top 100 leaders of the organization present) to work harder and innovate faster. He used a car metaphor and told the audience to "step on the gas." When he took questions from his people, one of the directors said to him that he struggled with the words of the CEO as he already had the feeling his team was "driving way above the speed limit." The CEO replied with a smile

and said that speed limits only count on public roads and their industry was on a racetrack. His advice to the director: "You have to go even faster!"

From a mental surplus point of view I very much prefer the approach of another client of mine, Aegon (an insurance, pensions, and asset management multinational). CEO Lard Friese explained to his people that he always works at 90%. Why? He explained it by saying he needs the extra 10% (the surplus) for an unexpected phone call (a crisis situation) when a boost of mental energy is needed. Now that is a future proof CEO!

Psychologists like Daniel Kahneman have concluded that being bored and dedicating time to dawdle is something we do less and less of but is vital for our mental health and creativity. I often get asked if 'getting bored' can be put on a to-do list, scheduled into an agenda or made into a KPI (key performance indicator). The answer is yes, that is a perfect starting point. So go and get bored – as soon as you've finished this book of course!

4. BUILD ROUTINES FIRST

One of the essential leadership skills of contemporary management literature is the quality to accept ambiguity and uncertainty, move agilely and constantly adapt to a rapidly changing world. Nothing is ever finished, everything is in a constant (or perpetual) beta[46] state. But how to do that mentally? From a business perspective it makes sense to be a dynamic, always adapting to change, super professional, but emotionally people also want calm, peace, rest and things to go as expected. That is why we have rituals and routines.

Often, when people become overworked and over-agiled (pun intended) only then do they seek rest. The concept of mental surplus is turning this around, meaning that the more

Mental surplus: one needs to
proactively invest in mental health
on a regular basis even if there seems
to be no need

ambiguity one has to deal with on a daily basis, the more rituals, patterns, and routines are needed to balance this out. A famous example of this is why Barack Obama always wore the same suits when he was president. His explanation: the decision to decide what to wear in the morning eroded his ability to make decisions later in the day.[47] A principle known in psychology as decision fatigue. This is also why a daily morning traffic jam is a calming routine for many commuters (compared to the maddening effect an unexpected traffic jam can have). It is in the routines and rituals we find rest and recharge our batteries.

It is time to turn the narrative around: start with building routines, practices, rituals as a way to create a mental surplus. Then the mental strength to manage ambiguity follows.

The higher a person's empathy skills, the lower their chances of a job burnout

5. FROM THE I TO THE WE

When Time Magazine put a mirror on its cover and made 'YOU' person of the year in 2006, they couldn't have been more right. Little did they know that social media with its likes, retweets, and shares – rocket fuelled by its algorithmic echo chambers – would mean even more emphasis on the I, the self, and the me.

The British author and actor, Stephen Fry, labels the era we live in the 'age of self', which did not start with social media, but ended with it. He places the start of this shift 150 years ago when god, king, church, country, city, town,

home, and family all came before the self. But this century 'self' has made it to the very top. And although Apple has claimed 'I' as the prefix of all its products, Fry sees 'self' as the prefix of our age. He offers a wonderful list of 'self' terms that illustrate the times we live in extremely well:

Self-help
Self-confidence
Self-assured
Self-publishing
Self-searching
Self-determination
Self-deprecation
Self-control
Self-esteem
Self-improvement
Self-satisfaction
Self-service
Self-awareness
Self-discipline
Self-knowledge
Self-seeking
Self-worth
Self-belief
Self-possession
Self-sacrifice
Self-image
Self-reliance
Self-expression
Self-denial
Self-assertion
Self-consciousness
Self-regard
Self-absorption
Self-obsession
Self-satisfaction
Self-righteousness
Self-centered
Self-loathing
Self-pity
Self-harm
Self-destruction
And…
Self-ies

Fry concludes his description of the era of self rather pessimistically with the observation that "we'd rather be individually right than at peace with each other."[48] French tech philosopher Éric Sadin goes one step further and says we now live in an era where we have become our own tyrant.[49] This is individualism taken to the extreme. It might be appealing to some, but we are inherently social animals and there is a wealth of research that shows it is our social connections, the social fabric of our lives, that is the key element in our happiness.

The Covid pandemic might just have been the wake-up call the world needed. Being locked down and forced to minimize social interactions had a huge impact on people's mental health.[50] Anyone who opened up a newspaper during the pandemic will have seen the alarming reports on the impact it has had on our mental well-being. All indicators – stress, sleeping disorders, anti-depressant usage, suicidal thoughts etc – were pointing in the wrong direction.[51] When asking my students during the pandemic what they missed most, the top answer, by a wide margin, was always, getting together with their friends, hugging them, going to festivals.

The age group that suffered mentally the least during the pandemic were people in their forties and fifties. These were the people with their social fabric at its peak. Most have found a life partner and made their friends for life. Most have an established professional network and high engagement with colleagues they have been working with in physical proximity for many years. And last but not least, many have children at home.[52] Most leaders fall in this age group and it's of vital importance for them to empathize with the other age groups on this front.

Covid will hopefully prove to be a life lesson for the long term, where people realize the importance of the 'we' over the 'I'. The short term response after the lockdowns was that of one big social-party-festive-travel-get-together

because "I suffered so much." The long term might be more of a focus on the collective. Organizations can play into this as well, by focussing on teams, groups, and boosting the social relationship between their employees. This creates a mental surplus before the next crisis hits, whether it is a new pandemic, an economic crisis, or a disruptive natural disaster.

6. GET OUTSIDE HELP

And last, but not least, get outside help in improving your mental health. A self-help book or YouTube course might work for some, but most people benefit best from the help of a real human being. Currently there is a proliferation of (online) mental help professionals and I often encounter leaders who are confused by all the psychologists, therapists, coaches, mentors, and counselors offering services and support. Please be patient here; as time passes the mental health industry will become more organised and accredited in similar ways to the physical health industry. For the time being don't be afraid to ask your youngest employees for advice.

Help can also be offered from inside an organization. More and more organizations offer some form of mental health support to their people. And this trend has been accelerated by Covid. Mental health support at work has been around for decades, but is now taken more seriously. And mental health professionals have gotten cool names like Chief Well-being Officer.[53] Some of my clients are employing mental health professionals. An accountancy firm I work with employed four full-time psychologists to support their personnel. They have opened up a dedicated mental health helpline and they recently shifted to measuring employee well-being on a weekly basis. The mental surplus shift means that these professionals are not there to help employees only when they experience mental health problems, but to create a permanent culture that fosters mental well-being for everyone, all the time.

STRATEGIC TAKEAWAY

Organizations and their leaders have to create a culture of mental surplus. This means that employees have an excess of mental health, so drawbacks in work or personal life can be absorbed. This means leaders have to proactively build that mental surplus, for themselves and for their people.

ACKNOWLEDGEMENTS

This book would not have been written without the support of my friends, family, and colleagues. I want to thank Femke, Diede, and Loewe for making all my writing struggles seem trivial. The original idea to materialize all my thinking into a book came from Cosimo Turroturro. Thank you for being my mentor since 2013 and for your patience on this one.

I very much appreciate all those who have given invaluable feedback on the content: Bas Delmee, Monte Königs, Matthew Smith, Selese Roche, and Tess Czerski.

Thank you to Meredith Norwich and Chloe Herbert at Routledge for publishing the book; my literary agent Kizzy Thomson for guiding me on this journey; and Regine Dugardyn for all your wisdom. And a standing ovation for graphic designer and creative mastermind David Pino for making this book stand out!

I founded Whetston / strategic foresight in 2014 and many of the insights in this book are inspired by our work with many clients. I would like to thank all those who have hired me as a speaker, trainer, and consultant. Without you, this book wouldn't exist – you have given me so many invaluable stories and experiences. I can't name all of the people I have worked with, but I can mention the organizations:

Santander, Russell, Google, PVH, Finn, Roschier, ECB, ULI, DLA Piper, Abbott, Coloplast, IKEA, Fujitsu, NEP, ASVB, Microsoft, Bunge, Vodafone, Spar, E.ON, Academi Wales, Regal, Zurich, Aegon, Finastra, Croonwolter&dros, Invesco, AMEC, Latvia Tourism, Hartwall Oy, Synergi, Confinn, Citywire, Ingenico, Hydrosol, ABN AMRO, Ingenico, Oracle, Vistage, Plan International, JP Morgan, Nesta, CHP, Dustin, Centiro, Podiem, MGI, VMware, Verse, Tomra, Stedin, Nore HR, Swedbank, Accountor, Nike, Technopolis, CLIA, Dunedin, L'Oreal, Danfoss, The Hunt, Exambela, GX, BCO, Deloitte, Bottega Veneta, Janssen, Crowe, KWF, Booking, GSK, OTE, Dropbox, Cybersource, SRM, Primark, Oliver Wight, Bambora, HSE, MFS, RVDB, Kelloggs, Gultaggen, Avis, Tarmac, BNP Paribas, IFT, ISLEXPO, Novartis, Cielo, EPDA, BNY Mellon, FTI, Europulp, Stena, Ster, Abloy, Intertrust, OxfordSM, Atea, Atrium, BGL, iLOQ, Çalik Denim, Visa, Tungsten, COOP, RBS, TedX, Nixu, HvA, Veidekke, Eneco, Learning Conference, JCP, Fingerprints, Sanofi, Symetri, Turku Business School, Gala, Tridium, Uponor, PostNL, HCL, Lexmundi, Sabre, Northern Glow, Stora Enso, Learnfest, Virke, Honeywell, Warner, Kauppakeskusyhdistyksen, Diebold Nixdorf, Mediaforum, EY, Guldgalan, Bloomreach, Luxottica, Adecco, Randstad, Entraforum, Generali, Opus Capita, SEB, Talentum, Beeline, Miltton, Nordic Morning, F5, II, UWV, Ace & Company, Ferring, Scania, BDIA, Nordic Shopping, Macquarie, Merck, NEC, Ball, Ericsson, Kiinteistöalan, Helkama, Mills & Reeve, Buyin, ICC, Morgan Stanley, MWG, MDV, Rabobank, Telia, 30Mhz, Tieto, Ici Paris XL, Skanska, CIEE, EPTDA, IMI, Wolters Kluwer, RTL, Prosales, Tetra Pak, HZPC, IIEX, Acuro, VNU, HSBC, Reply, MDV, Hay, KLM, Leroy Merlin, Land Securities, OMD, Luxinnovation, Aetna, Buehler, UFI & Hewlett Packard.

REFERENCES

INTRODUCTION

1   2   3

1. BLURRING REALITIES

1   2   3   4   5   6

7   8   9   10   11   12

13   14   15   16   17   18

19   20[1]   20[2]   20[3]   21   22

23 24 25 26 27 28

29 30[1] 30[2] 31 32 33

34 35 36[1] 36[2] 37 38

39 40 41 42 43 44

45 46 47 48 49 50

51 52 53 54

2. TRUST PENDULUM

1 2 3 4 5 6

55   56   57   58

3. YOU KNOW ME

1   2   3¹   3²   3³   4

5   6   7   8   9   10

11   12   13   14   15   16

17

4. DIGITAL BALANCE

1   2   3   4   5   6

5. FUTURE ETHICS

1	2	3	4	5	6
7	8	9	10	11	12
13	14	15	16	17	18
19	20	21	22	23	24
25	26	27	28	29	30
31	32	33	34	35	36
37	38	39	40	41	42

43   44   45   46   47   48

49

6. MENTAL SURPLUS

1   2   3   4   5   6

7   8   9   10   11   12

13   14   15   16   17   18

19   20   21   22   23   24

25   26   27   28   29   30

31 32 33 34 35 36

37 38 39 40 41 42

43 44 45 46 47 48

49 50 51 52 53

If you have stumbled upon a QR-code with a dead link, please send an email to info@whetston.com and we'll fix it straight away, thanks and have a wonderful day!